newoman

THE SURVIVAL GUIDE

newoman

TO GROWING OLDER

ROSAMOND RICHARDSON

A powerful and empowering book for and about older women

KYLE CATHIE LIMITED

Acknowledgements

With special thanks to Vanessa Webster, Vicki Culverwell, and to my sister Dr Juliet Compston, as well as to many friends for their input and feedback during the writing of this book. Thanks also to Jenny Joseph for permission to quote from her poem 'Warning' (page 193).

First published in Great Britain in 2001 by
Kyle Cathie Limited,122 Arlington Road, London NW1 7HP

ISBN 1 85626 405 X

Text © 2001 Rosamond Richardson
Photography © 2001 Michelle Garrett

Editor Sheila Davies · Copy editor Anne Newman · Designer Heidi Baker

Rosamond Richardson is hereby identified as the author of this work in accordance with Section 77 of the Copyright, Designs and Patents Act 1988.

A CIP catalogue record for this title is available from the British Library.

Printed and bound in Singapore.

For all new women, everywhere

contents

introduction

We are always the same age inside Gertrude Stein

As the 21st century dawns over Western society, a silent revolution is taking place. For the first time in history, older people outnumber the young. But the trouble is that many of them don't *feel* old. It comes as a constant surprise to them to be described as such by those who still subscribe to outdated stereotypes. But increasingly, as the circle of this revolution turns, younger generations do not perceive older people in the same light as their predecessors did, they do not see them as being as old as their years. Grandmothers used to be little old ladies with white hair and arthritis, sitting in chairs knitting by the fire. Now they are gorgeous women of any age from 30-something upwards who keep fit down the gym. There is a saying that today's 60 is yesterday's 40: we stay younger longer (with any luck).

A hundred years ago, average life expectancy was 30 years less than it is today. The vital question now arises as to how to live those years in order to get the best from them.

In today's world our real age is not counted in numbers: it is the way we feel that defines us. Being healthier, wealthier and better educated than any other generation in history helps us to wear our years lightly: this means that a new kind of life begins after 50. Many of us find that 50-plus no longer feels at all like the downhill slide it was supposed to be. If the clichés about 50 being younger than it used to be are true, then equally untrue are the 'over the hill' ones. Fifty no longer means the scrapheap. The New Woman (as opposed to the Old Woman) is now liberated from the stereotype of the old fogey (unless of course she indulges the irony of consciously becoming one, as a kind of revenge). Age has become an adventure rather than a catalogue of decay. The redefinition of the older contemporary woman as 'new' has no room even for patronising epithets like 'silver surfers' or 'grey power'. She is free to refute such labels as firmly as she may choose to defy categorisation.

However, turning 50 can be a bit like getting to the edge of the world (the flat version) and falling off into the void. Where is the map? As we emerge over the horizon of middle age, many of us blink in bewilderment at the blank landscape. Where are the signposts that point the way through this uncharted territory? Because actually the world is round, there *is* terra firma beyond that horizon of middle age, a territory that we are gradually, fumblingly clarifying as our collective lives get longer.

For many of us, 50 symbolises a new beginning – but the beginning of what? The path has no map. We have inherited maps, roughly speaking, for childhood, puberty and adolescence in Act One of our lives, for work, career, marriage, children and for the middle years of Act Two, but what about Act Three? Ethel Barrymore said that a good life is like a good play: it has to have a satisfying and exciting third act. Well, maybe it is up to us to write the script.

An ageing population is a testament to progress. The reason why 'older people' are not ready to be consigned to the rubbish dump is because their bodies and minds have thrived on better nutrition and healthcare, and more universal and lifelong education, than that which was available to their parents. However, some elements in society have moved more slowly than the turning wheel of the silent revolution and have not exactly welcomed them with open arms. The phrase 'demographic timebomb' is usually used negatively, yet the

vitality of the so-called 'baby-boomers' (alluding to the soaring birth rate just after the Second World War) could turn what could be a problem of an 'ageing society' into a positive advantage. Maturity has its own riches, which can profitably be ploughed back into its soil; but age discrimination dies hard. However, it is likely to be in its death throes as women surge over the 50-plus horizon, unimpeded by outdated concepts of ageism. The revolution will become less silent as they creatively chart – and not without humour – a new map for these unprecedented years of possibility.

Many cultures and civilisations have venerated age: for North American Indians it formed the basis for rank and precedence. The ancient civilisations of China, Sparta, Greece and Rome have left in their modern counterparts residues of respect for the 'elders', still evident in their cohesive family structures. In African and Polynesian cultures the old woman is often the wise woman. In India, it is a Hindu tradition to devote the last quarter of life to inner development and spiritual contemplation. Around the world 'elders' have traditionally been revered, their wisdom harvested. Age is seen as a privilege and appreciated as borrowed time.

For women today, the quality of this new lease of life may be linked to the material practicalities of everyday life, to relationships, to work or leisure, to health, or to enriching the mind or to the numinous. Jung describes a 'psychology of the morning of life and a psychology of the afternoon'. A spiritual landscape opens out for older people, one whose existence is often denied or scorned by a prevalently consumer-oriented culture. We can decide for ourselves whether it is of value, we can connect with it or not, that is our choice, but whatever we decide to do with these years, it is time for us to draw our own map for vital ageing.

The recognition and inclusion of the potential, the experience and the vitality peculiar to the 'older person' have vast implications for society as a whole, implications that have not escaped the notice of politicians. The 'grey vote' (hideous expression) is a potent force. Nearly half of the electorate in the UK is now aged over 50, and similar patterns are emerging in other Western societies. Many of them are as articulate as they are demanding. For the first time ever, people over 50 demand policies to improve their circumstances: with the weight of numbers in their favour, they now have the power to vote in the politicians who will give them what they want, and to vote out those who fail them.

We have arrived at a new place on the wheels of this silent revolution. It is up to this generation of older women to insist on being heard and become visible in society – as many are already doing – to walk the talk, to change things and to provide an example to those who will follow. Today's older women are the ones who can transform the quality of our new longer lives. Creating a fresh archetype of the 'new woman' is the responsibility of this age.

the new woman

the new woman

We turn older with the years, but newer every day Emily Dickinson

Something wonderful can happen when you turn 50. The fact is that you can design your own process of ageing: age need only be a trajectory of decomposition if you allow it to be. Successful ageing, however, doesn't mean living in denial and faking youthfulness, it means staying active mentally, physically, psychologically and socially. Either we make the choices to remain so, or we opt to become victims of the concept of 'age' that is fuelled by stereotypes. 'Be courageous,' says Anita Roddick, founder of the Body Shop and now in her late 50s. 'It's one of the few places left uncrowded.'

For me, 50 was a watershed. I felt like I'd climbed a mountain and could turn through 360 degrees to see all around me, and the view from the midpoint (possibly) of my life was great. It gave me a perspective on all my adventures and failures and loves and disasters. Halfway through my personal century I was ready to put down some of the equipment that had got me this place, and to travel lighter. This freedom, as it turned out, happened to be a key that opened many doors. As a joke I decided to count my next 50 years backwards to zero, and since then I have felt more carefree, healthier, stronger and more alive than at any other age. Even though my birthday suit requires ironing I get more intense pleasure out of daily life now than ever before. It has been more of a beginning than an ending, probably because I decided it would.

Outdated stereotypes of 'older people' – comic-strip cartoon caricatures of fat, decrepit, bad-tempered, dependent, useless women wielding umbrellas threateningly, or hell's grannies brandishing handbags, or pathetic, negative old women who whinge – are rooted in history. The Elizabethan wit Francis Bacon poured scorn on those old people 'who object too much, consult too long, adventure too little, and repent too soon'. That we still believe in them is due to our

conditioning, fuelled by the ageism endemic in society at many levels.

Stereotypes die hard even though academic research indicates that these popular myths are unfounded in reality. The Center on Ageing at the University of Maryland found that children of all ages had negative attitudes about (but limited knowledge of) older people. They perceived them as helpless, unhealthy, not alert, needing support, lonely and poor, leading boring lives and being less intelligent and informed that they were. However, less than a quarter could name a single older person outside the family and were basing their views on stereotypes rather than on actual contact with older people. Yet such children would quite happily admire vintage film stars.

We do not have to bow to the authority of demeaning archetypes. Our bones do not have to creak, nor must our libido decline, or our zest for life diminish as the years go by. Whether they do or not is entirely up to us. We can if we want to side-step that conditioning and choose to remain active and healthy as we grow older. Science and medicine are on our side, but the most powerful tool of all is a positive attitude. It is time to dump stereotypes, to create new archetypes and to be positive role models for our children – who are likely to live even longer than we are.

Fifty onwards is *not* a Twilight Zone. It is not the zone of the expanding waistline and narrowing mind, of shrinking tolerance and withdrawal from the world into a grey tunnel where everything slows down and everyone goes faster than you. Or at any rate it does not have to be. We are all free to make the choice as to whether to stay eager, interested and open-minded, or whether to settle into negative ways, and to give up developing our potential. Jeanne Moreau, whose beauty is as much in her intelligence and personality as in her physical looks, says, 'The older you get, the more you realise that everything is the fruit of what you are.' And the poet May Sarton is quoted as having said on her 70th birthday, 'I am more myself than ever.'

If there is a problem, it has to do with labelling: 'old' is usually an insult. Labels are potent because they describe how we think about someone, and what we think about someone influences how they behave. If someone sees you as 'fuddy-duddy' or 'frumpy' or 'middle-aged' or a 'senior citizen', this affects how you react with them, it influences your behaviour, and consequently your place in *their* scheme of things. In *The Fountain of Age* Betty Friedan quotes a US Harris Poll in which only 8 per cent of the over-65s found 'old' an acceptable adjective. They objected strongly to 'old-timer', 'retired person', 'golden-ager'. 'Grey' and 'silver' are equally ghastly, and as for the tongue-in-cheek 'chronically gifted'...? Please.

No. 'New Woman' is more like it. This comes far closer to Emily Dickinson's truth (see page 14) than the tag of 'Old Woman'. Let's face it, which would you prefer to be known as?

Active planning for this stage of life opens up its many possibilities, and for this we need information.

Some facts and figures

Average life expectancy in Western societies has increased by almost 30 years since 1900.

Eighty per cent of all centenarians are women. By 2050 there will be 2 million (mostly female) in the USA.

Swedish figures for 1998 show that of people aged over 95, 8240 were women, and 2156 men.

Nearly half (44 per cent) of older white Americans, 60 per cent of blacks and 57 per cent of Hispanics, say that these are the best years of their lives, according to a national survey conducted in 1999, and 84 per cent of all Americans say they would be happy to live to 90.

Swedish statistics forecast that the number of women aged between 100 and 104 will rise from 2038 in 2010, to 5141 in 2050.

Since 1900 the number of people over 60 worldwide has increased by 400 per cent, and doubled since 1931.

There is no compulsory retirement age in the USA. Sweden and the UK are considering raising theirs from 65 to 67.

By 2010 there will be as many seniors as there are people aged under 20: by 2020 every second European adult out of a population of 130 million will be over 50.

People born between 1946 and 1964 account for 25 per cent of the US population. By 2020, due to falling birth rates, they will make up 35 per cent. In the UK in 2000 'baby-boomers' numbered 9 million in a population of 52 million.

Of Swedish centenarian women in 1998, 245 were widows, 56 were unmarried, 9 were divorced and 4 married.

Boomer-consumers: the 50-plus population owns 77 per cent of all financial assets in the USA. This is power! By 2005 50 per cent of people aged over 50 will have the highest discretionary income of any generation in history.

According to a Royal Commission report of 1999, the population of over-80s in Europe is projected to have risen by 2050 by at least 200 per cent, in the USA by 800 per cent, in the UK around 250 per cent.

In 1996 a woman of 60 in Western society could expect to live a further 22 years.

Women aged between 55 and 59 account for 6 per cent of the European workforce (1997) and 8 per cent of women aged 60 and over were still in employment.

By 2031 there will be 5000 centenarians in the UK alone, most of whom will be women.

Information gives us the power to change things: armed with information we can reassess, make new discoveries, and go in new directions, and that is the aim of this book. Making the decision to *act* is the first step on this trajectory. 'Women in advancing old age,' said the novelist Dorothy Sayers, 'are unstoppable by any earthly force.'

Gird up your self-esteem and identify what it is you would love to do. Break open the shell of your conditioning and emerge into your full potential. Visualise your dreams. Write them down. Draw your own map. Create a new role for yourself. Whatever courage you need to take these new steps, to take risks even, summon it to seek new challenges. The rewards are great: you could revitalise your mind, reinvent yourself, and transform the rest of your life.

Demolishing some of the myths

Categorising older women is becoming increasingly difficult; it is not so easy to slot them into some 'grey and wrinkly' department where they will behave in ways expected of them. Today, 50-plus women are as likely to be doing the school run as they are struggling to help their teenagers with their exams. They may be embarking on a new career, or a new marriage. They may be enjoying active grandparenthood, travelling around the world for the United Nations, running the marathon, or writing their first best-seller. The prevailing myths look horribly past their sell-by date: that, by definition, older women

- are forgetful, slow mentally and physically, frail, ill, lonely, ugly, fat, boring
- are complacent and set in their ways
- play golf and bridge
- don't have sex
- are no longer numerate and literate and can be ripped off and conned into anything
- are unable to read irony and sycophancy in others
- are cynical and negative
- have low self-esteem

It's hard to take seriously.

Nearer the truth is that older women today know that their chronological age is the least important defining factor of their lives. Rather, this increasingly dynamic age group knows that attitude is all.

Our perception is our reality. How we see the world, the model of the world with which we operate, is, to us, 'reality'. To someone else it is something else. These patterns of thinking, usually in place by the time we are between five and seven years old, are the product of early childhood conditioning. To a great extent we are what we think, and the key to our lives is that we have the power to change our thoughts. Once we see our conditioning for what it is, we are free to dictate our own lives. 'Nothing,' as Shakespeare so adroitly put it, 'is good or bad but thinking makes it so.' Our lives are the creation of our minds.

Only outdated visions of what age entails can impede our trajectory into the fulfilment of maturity, the accomplishment of our full potential, and to our ability to change and adapt to circumstances. 'What one needs, my dear,' said my 103-year-old friend to me recently, 'is a certain amount of elasticity.' She should know. Women like her are not just flexible, they are resilient, they are strong. In any case 'age' starts much later than it used to. A UK government think-tank called itself 'The Debate of the Age' in recognition of the importance of demographic change and its implications (see Resources, page 202). And at the launch of the International Year of the Older Person in 1999, Kofi Annan, the UN Secretary General, said, 'changing demographics have created a "silent revolution" with major economic, social, cultural, psychological and spiritual implications.'

We have the opportunity to implement that revolution. So far from being the weaker sex, we live longer than men and thus have the biological advantage. We can demonstrate that age is a privilege, and that it is also a state of mind. Part of this change entails drawing a new map of our lifespan, not as a single downhill track, but as a sequence of stages, all of them with different qualities and all of them valuable. As we as individuals transform this new thinking into experience, so our families and friends will be influenced by our example. The effect of this could be a gradual erosion of ageism which would then permeate through to society and the media, until a time comes when older people are viewed as capable, valuable and independent. The energy of experience and the serenity of maturity can be ploughed back into society, manuring the soil for the next generation. We will be acknowledged as the strong and accomplished citizens that we have the potential to be in this exciting phase of our lives.

The psychology of ageing

Studies show that women continue to gain in psychological maturity well into their 60s and 70s. However, ageing is not a singular process: we age biologically and sociologically as well as psychologically, and the ageing experience is determined by the interactions between all these three factors.

Drawing parallels between young and old age groups casts an interesting light on what appear at first sight to be diametrically opposed states, yet both are times of mental and physical change and they have more in common than meets the eye. Both are often characterised by an increase in introspection, a need for meaning, the questioning of identity and the tensions between solitude, loneliness and a sense of privacy with a need to interrelate to society. Crucially, as Simone de Beauvoir points out in her *Coming of Age*, it is the meaning that we attribute to our lives, our entire system of values, that define the meaning and value of our older age – just as it did in our youth.

Part of the problem of perception of older people is to do with roles. Roles shape our identity, and affect the orientation of those with whom we interact. Social roles are as much defined by age as they are by gender, class and race. They are legitimised by socio-psychological models that are often age-graded: 'What do you do?' is a social question quickly followed by an (often deeply unconscious) assessment of age which is part and parcel of a judgement about that person's usefulness or lack of it. Each age has its assumed appropriate role-performance: youth, courtship and marriage, career, childbearing, parenting. Lost in this game plan is the new phenomenon of the extra 30 years granted to us by better health and hygiene. A century ago women usually did not have the opportunities, the health, the education or simply the luck to connect to the essential and potential person that they were beyond their sexual and reproductive destiny, or the freedom to see themselves as more

than that. Stereotypes ruled the day. This new stage of the life cycle remains undefined and its roles are partly obscured by our collective guilt about doing what fulfils us. Does 50-plus mean a marginalised wasteland inhabited by spectres of outdated stereotypes? The choice is ours.

Since society provides us with no recipes for appropriate behaviour and goals, we can and must create our own subculture with its distinctive norms and values. Turn your 50th birthday into a major cause for celebration. Create a new rite of passage into this regenerated 'older age', into the potentially fertile lands of maturity. Create a ritual like the festivities for the crucial events of birth, puberty, marriage, childbirth and death. Throw a great party to mark the menopause, dance the night away and celebrate a new life. Rituals are empowering: you might feel like having a great bonfire to burn stuff you don't want or need in your life any more. Or you might choose to go on the trip of a lifetime to somewhere you have always dreamed of going, or of spending a day in a hot air balloon or paragliding. If this wonderful new phase of life is not celebrated, then older women will always occupy a secondary place in our social system. They will remain marginalised, not only to their own detriment but also to the detriment of others who will lose out on a vast resource of energy and experience that can be ploughed back into society.

By attaching significance to age, older people can help to shape the meaning of the human life cycle. The unique capacity of the older ones to see how past, present and future interact provides a fertile inheritance for the young. Intelligent and open-hearted older people know their debt to the past and from that springs their obligation to their children and chldren's children.

In many modern societies, however, age is often doubly stigmatised for women, who are perceived to be obsolete earlier than men, both sexually and in the workplace. Age discrimination works overtime against women: to be silver-haired and craggy is 'distinguished' if you are male, 'elderly' (and by implication over the hill) if you are female. Traditional male-dominated perceptions of femininity (inherited by females too to some extent) involve incompetence, helplessness, non-competitiveness and passivity. Ageism and sexism march hand in hand. Today's mature women have to turn this around and show that there is no need for them to conform to the 'dependent and useless' stereotype of the doddering and infirm elderly. After all, the dependency of the past is neutralised by the fact of feeling younger and healthier. We are able to keep working and active in society. And if we choose not to work, unemployment is not a category specific to older people, since by no means are all those of 'working age' in employment: it happens to the young, too.

The challenges being mounted to this paradigm by today's 'older women', those who are choosing to grow old disgracefully, are timely. Actions speak louder than words: a positive and active view of ageing can permeate and transform the collective consciousness. In *As You like It* Jacques cynically describes the sixth age of the seven ages of man as beslippered, bespectacled, shrunken and enfeebled. His 'ages of man' are a far cry from the modern metamorphosis of women. Wouldn't Shakespeare be surprised if he visited the 21st century and bumped into the 'never too old' brigade of feisty, energetic and enterprising women who have refused to accept such stereotypes of decrepitude and who instead are flying solo around the world in a helicopter like 60-year-old grandmother Jennifer Murray (*The Times*, June 2000), writing their first best-selling novel at 60 like Penelope Fitzgerald did, seeing Sydney on a Harley-Davidson like Sally Greengross, then 65, with only one and a half hours in the city before her flight departed, or Helen Thayer who at 52 skied to the magnetic North Pole pulling a 72kg (160lb) sled for 27 days over a distance of 555km (345 miles), meeting polar bears, running into blizzards and surviving near-starvation and a period of blindness and emerging, in her own word, 'reborn'.

Keys to healthy ageing

Age may mean wrinkles and grey hairs but it does not have to mean diminishing intelligence, lack of interest, increased pessimism, a pot-belly or stiffening joints. The key to vital ageing is to maintain your capacity for mindful control. Successful ageing is an attitude, and an art also, the art of using your mental and physical abilities to the full and embracing your full potential as a human being. You can remain lively, cheerful, lucid, trim and mobile into your later years – if you choose to, and if you work at it. You may need luck on your side; but the Chinese say there are two kinds of luck; the kind you are born with and the kind you make yourself – and with the latter, the more you practise, the luckier you get. We are born with our genes, but the key factors of health and environment are also to some degree influenced by our own thoughts and actions.

Some Keys
(Available to All, and Free)

• **A positive attitude**
Repeatedly, international studies show that people who are optimistic, assertive, and who do not dwell on things even in times of stress live to a greater age than those whose outlook is more negative. Try to see age as a possibility rather than as a limitation: it may provide something you had never thought of as being available to you. Keeping an unshakeable interest in life is another characteristic of successful ageing.

• **Being ready to rise to new challenges of any kind**
New challenges might include relationships, work, your body, your mind, creativity, your spiritual life, travel etc. Allow no limits on your curiosity, welcome new adventures, and indulge your thirst for novelty. Life is wonderfully

exciting, and it's worth taking the risk of stepping outside known parameters.

• **Laughing a lot**
Have fun. Develop your sense of humour; it is a great stress-buster. Research into centenarians shows that they deal well with tragic events that might devastate the less optimistic, bouncing back from the inevitable pain and stress of life with a positive attitude. Katharine Hepburn said at the age of 83 (still standing on her head daily and plunging into the lake for a swim), 'I think everything's quite funny. Laughing is fun and I laugh at practically everything.'

• **Staying sociable**
It is well documented that lonely people suffer more depression and ill health than those who stay connected with friends and community. My friend Nina was widowed in her late 70s after a long marriage dominated by her husband which had left her little space for her own interests. She took up with the local church, joined a bridge group, went swimming every week with a friend, and frequently has visitors – of all ages – to stay. She often goes to the theatre with friends at the ripe old age of 91. Other women I know have taken up voluntary work or joined special interest groups, which has kept their spirits high.

• **Good physical and mental health**
Although luck may not always be on our side,

we can help ourselves to a great extent. Looking after our health from the age of 40 upwards is the greatest investment we can make in our lives. This means eating healthily, taking sensible exercise even if you have never done so before, even if it is just walking or swimming. Regular physical activity keeps both body and brain functional and vigorous. Keep stretching. Physical exercise becomes more, not less important as you age, to maintain strength and muscle. It helps to burn fat, reduces the risk of heart disease and substantially improves your sense of well-being.

Continue to meet mental challenges: mental exercise keeps you fit too since the brain is a muscle and brain cells can die of boredom. Mental training slows the ageing of the brain. Keep those grey cells stimulated (the majority of centenarians do, according to the figures); take up a second or third career and a new stimulating hobby. Use it or lose it!

- **Being non-conformist**
  Break the mould. Break away from stereotypes and do what you want (within reason) – the stimulation to your brain keeps it active (see Brain Power, page 56–71). Stay eager, lively, interested and broad-minded. You never know, it may be your last chance

- **Don't smoke**
  No smoking. Simple. Just don't. If you do, give it up. Now (see page 118).

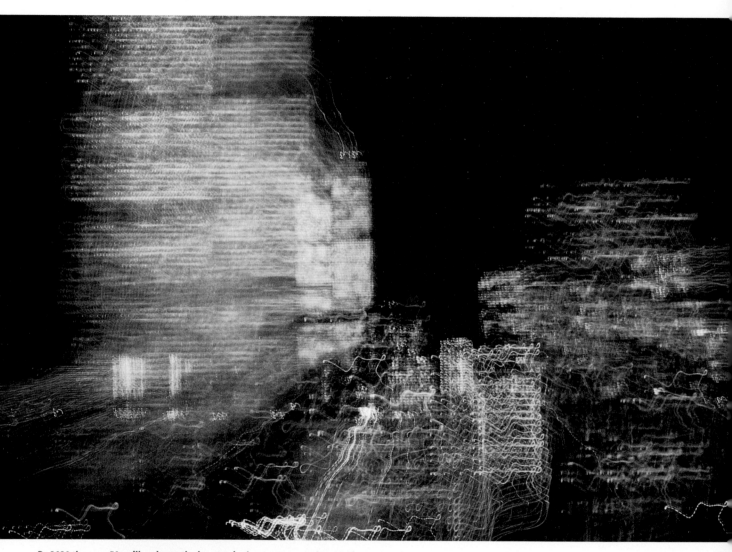

By 2020 the over-50s will make up the largest single consumer market ever known.

Issues of social and political power

Halfway through the 20th century Simone de Beauvoir pointed out that the increasingly large group of older people in society were failing to integrate into the community: 'Society,' she wrote in *Coming of Age*, 'is compelled to decide upon their status, and the decision can only be taken at government level. Old age has become the subject of policy.' This however turned out to be truer in the USA than it was in Europe: the 1965 Older American Act is, effectively, a Bill of Rights for the elderly. It seeks to guarantee an adequate income, best possible healthcare, suitable housing, institutional care, opportunities for employment, a dignified retirement commensurate with the individual's contribution to society, access to meaningful recreational and cultural activities, efficient community services, and personal freedom and independence in managing their own lives. Sounds perfect. Indeed, what other age group can claim such entitlements?

But which other political systems have emulated this lead? It is only now, at the beginning of the 21st century, that the UK government is even considering a 'ministry of grey power' (hideous title) headed by a cabinet minister, to look at whether the over-55s could be more active in community and voluntary work, as well as offering incentives to businesses to keep older people in employment. Whereas the USA, pioneering the way ahead, now has an 'ageing network' (equally hideous name) to sustain the principles of the 1965 act, and has among other things abolished mandatory retirement limits. The Americans have been quick to understand that age is an opportunity rather than a difficulty to be overcome. Thus new models of ageing are based on vitality, activity and autonomy, offering possibilities for self-fulfilment, for valuing people as much for what they are as what they do, and seeing the value of experience as a useful counterweight to the prevailing cult of youth.

Only now is it beginning to dawn on the European mind that it may be a good idea to develop products and services for older people, not only to help them retain their independence but in order to buoy up the economy. This is because it has become clear that this increasingly healthy and active group has substantial spending power. Studies of Europe-wide sales have shown that the over-50s buy 80 per cent of the top-of-the-range cars, 60 per cent of the olive oil, 55 per cent of the coffee, 50 per cent of the face-lift cosmetics, 50 per cent of the mineral water, 50 per cent of the yoghurt, and 35 per cent of travel! By 2020 the over-50s will make up the largest single consumer market ever seen (every other one of 130 million Europeans will fall into this age group). This staggering number will command an increasing proportion of wealth and disposable income. The current age barrier that operates, causing advertisers, retailers and manufacturers to shun the concept of 'older', results in them shooting themselves in the foot. The fact is, statistically, that the youth market is declining in numbers while the older end of the market is ready to boom.

Economic power is political power. The new woman is aware of this power and wants to use it, and this has not gone unnoticed by politicians everywhere. The over-55s vote with a vengeance: in 1996 a *New York Times* poll found that the over-60s cast 24 per cent of the total vote. This percentage will increase as more educated cohorts move into this age bracket. In the UK it has been found that the over-55s are the most likely to vote in a general election (over 80 per cent of the over-50s voted in the 1997 election, whereas only 57 per cent of the 16-34s did so).

There is power in numbers. This power has a substantial female quotient (because women live longer, on average, than men do), and its strength was illustrated by an incident in June 2000, when Britain's prime minister, Tony Blair, was heckled by the massed forces of the doughty women of the Women's Institute. The front-page headline in *The Times* the next day read, 'WI puts Tony Blair in his place'. As he began to give a party-political speech to this non-political, non-sectarian organisation, they spontaneously heckled him and began a slow handclap. Lost for words and deeply embarrassed, he stumbled his way through the offending script and retired hurt. He and his advisers had not taken into account the confident energy of these women who knew that they had the authority to articulate their views and be heard. Over the previous half-century they had had a considerable influence on government and

were not going to be messed with. They had been vocal in areas of equal pay, better conditions for nurses, clean air and pollution, cruelty and neglect of children, battered women, pensions for carers, AIDS education, cloning, GM foods, adult education, issues around farming and food production, and the saving of rural post offices. They were and are a force to be reckoned with and they knew it. This is political power. Any 'ministry of grey power' may need to look at ceasing to patronise women and to defer to their experience and special brand of wisdom.

The growing political power of women raises in turn issues of age-neutrality. Discrimination on the grounds of age, 'ageism', is endemic in many countries, particularly towards women. It is up to the new women of our times to change this, to redefine values and attitudes and to find an antidote to the poison of ageism by emulating the example of such leading lights as the women quoted in this book, in order to alter ingrained prejudice. This is not as easy as it sounds: but the people who have succeeded in doing so are largely people who have ignored ageist attitudes and just got on with what they want to do. Brush it aside and do yourself a favour.

With the weight of numbers on our side of the balance, if we go down so does the community, whereas if we engage in an active and vital 'third age', the bloodstream of society will be oxygenated by our energy. We are all a part of this challenge, because if there is only one thing of which we can be certain, it is that we are all growing older.

Economic power is political power.

freedom!

freedom!

*When you are young everything
is about you. As you grow older,
and are pushed to the margin,
you begin to realise that everything
is not about you, and that is the
beginning of freedom* Germaine Greer

Women's lives often take off at 50-plus. When Elizabeth Taylor reached 60 she said, 'it is a great age to be. You can do things that are completely off the wall.' There is an Indian tradition that a baby girl is surrounded by 100 angels and a boy by 100 devils. Every year of their lives one of them swaps with another so that by the age of 100 all the devils are on the side of the woman. So after five decades of attending angelically to others' needs, the angel is beginning to be infiltrated by devils, allowing her to start looking after her own requirements. This stage of life is a great opportunity to find your wings and take flight in a spirit of confidence and

independence. The French call it 'a dangerous age'.

Doris Lessing describes the freedom of this stage of life: 'and then, not expecting it, you become middle-aged and anonymous. No one notices you, you achieve a wonderful freedom, it's a positive thing. You can move about, unnoticed and invisible.' We can turn this new invisibility into a real freedom, freedom from the focus on our sexual and reproductive potential.

This third stage on the map of our lives is a period that can last as long as childhood and adolescence put together. It can see the coming to fruition of neglected aspects of the psyche. Women of this age can be extraordinarily powerful, both politically and in their femininity. In late middle age Erica Jong said, 'I know what I want and who I am; I like myself. I delight in hearing what others have to say.' This is freedom from the necessary self-absorption of career years, freedom from the demands of bringing up a young family and learning (sometimes the hard way) about intense pair-bond relationships, and even deciding to be done with them.

Age is usually defined by number, but as the healthy lifespan of the majority increases in length, this becomes increasingly meaningless. Age would more usefully be defined by a decline in physical ability and loss of mental functioning, something that can happen at any age. Chronological age may not be a significant factor in determining, say, retirement age: health and wealth are more likely to influence our choice as to whether we work or decide to stop working. Health and (relative) wealth are also two key factors for most people in pursuing their personal ideas of what it means for their lives to go well. Both of these elements provide freedom and a level of autonomy which, in a society that respects human rights, are expected and respected by most individuals.

The freedoms available in this stage of life are manifold: freedom from the anxieties of childcare, or the pressures of full-time work, or the ambitions of upward mobility – or all of these put together. The freedom of not having to tolerate triviality if we don't want to, or continuing to see

people whose 'friendship' is as worn out as our old clothes. The freedom from having to apologise all the time, that straitjacket of guilt conditioning from which we can now break free. Although this is more difficult for some personalities than for others, the fact is that we can change our attitudes – gently, kindly – and this is freedom. Released from the success/failure business we can cast ambition and competitiveness among the lilies. The joys of grandchildren, of our adult children and relatives, and of new friends, can start to flourish. We can choose to pursue the work or leisure option that we always wanted to do but never had the time or opportunity. We are free to take up completely new challenges: 'You must,' said Eleanor Roosevelt, 'do the thing you think you cannot do.' Now is the time.

There is another kind of freedom too, the freedom from desire for material gain and acquiring possessions. Some older people, as statistics show (page 25) are happy to indulge in spending the relative wealth that can come with age, but a Canadian survey shows that there is also a proportion of this age group far less consumeristic than younger groups, in spite of their improved economic position in society. Their wish list was very small, if it existed at all. Asked what they would do if they won the lottery, most had great difficulty with the answer. They were by and large content with the status quo of the house and the car and the washing machine even if they were a little ragged around the edges, seeing length of ownership as added value, as a mark of

service, of relationship and continuity. Contentment was a word they used a lot.

The social psychologist Erik Erikson, who made a study of the lives of 70- and 80-year-olds, observed that it is at this age that one faces the supreme psychological challenges: challenges of acceptance of the past, the lessons of not blaming parents for being who they weren't, and oneself for not being someone 'better', forever wishing that they and we and others along the way had been different. This is the challenge of taking responsibility for past and future mistakes. The spirit of generous acceptance is a hallmark of maturity and results in a sense of personal liberation. Accepting imperfection, things as they are, opens the door to true serenity and may actually lead to a surge in energy as the psyche unlocks itself from the prison walls of unrealistic expectations and perfectionism.

For some, a definition of old age might be that of a person in spiritual decay. You can tell them a mile off by their whingeing voices and negative body-language, as opposed to those whose spirit remains alive and fresh. The latter are people who are true to themselves and are just who they are, defying old age, recognising that 'the pattern is new in every moment' (T. S. Eliot). We all recognise the ugliness of what Henry Miller called the 'putrefaction of the soul', where over-readiness to criticise, to self-pity, to be self-absorbed, narrow and rigid-minded hold sway as people grow older. My 103-year-old friend Nancy is a superb example of a shining spirit, despite the inevitable physical restrictions of being a centenarian (deafness but a good hearing aid, failing eyesight but good spectacles, and creaking joints about which there is not much to be done). Her memory is amazing, she is always *interested* (this is her secret) in people around her, she is unfailingly courteous and kind, and continues to follow her Quaker faith to sustain her. She is a wonderful listener and will remember the details of conversations we had months ago, which I may well have forgotten. She is still independent enough to live on her own in the home she has loved for nearly all her life, supported by a team of more than willing helpers who do shopping, cooking, gardening and cleaning – just because she is such a lovely person to be around. Her neighbour checks up on her every evening and drives her when she wants to go out. Her attitude to life is incredibly enthusiastic and wise, and combined as it is with insights Nancy has gained from a century of experience, provides a powerful example. She is a brilliant role model.

Nancy has made a point of cultivating not only her positive attitude but also her flexibility of mind. She has a great sense of humour and of the ridiculous, and has recovered from some enormous sorrows in her life with exemplary courage. Her attitude to death is as positive as her attitude to life. In contrast, I remember the once-beautiful blonde film star Anita Ekberg ranting and raging in a TV interview about the curse of ageing, the thickening of her waistline and her declining good looks. How ugly it made her appear. Simone de Beauvoir likewise, used to living her life through Jean-Paul Sartre, fumed in vain at the loss of her attractiveness, at the sagging face and heavy chin that she met daily in the mirror. Colette spent futile hours trying to conceal her ageing face under cakes of make-up, and her lost figure under flowing garments. Disgusted by her body and showing it to no one but her maid, she ended up lonely. In contrast, Nancy's acceptance of and appreciation of what life has handed her, her enjoyment of each day, makes her – wrinkles and bent back notwithstanding – more beautiful than any of these iconic women.

Such wonderful freedoms may not be bought cheaply. We may have patterns of thinking that get in the way, entrenched views of our place in the world needing to be a particular way that are an obstacle to this psychological and spiritual freedom. Lethargy may be an impediment: we cannot be bothered to make the effort. But this is the age at which healthy self-examination can be constructive not just for us but for those around us. We may discover patterns of thinking that we dislike, and want to change. It's a mistake to believe that the old dog cannot learn new tricks (you are undermining your own intelligence as well as that of our four-legged friends). If you decide to do something, you can do it. It is up to *you*. If you find yourself thinking, 'It's no good, I can't change myself after all these years,' change your thinking to, 'I can do this. I want to change. I haven't peaked yet. Everything is possible.' This is freedom, and it comes from your mind, from the way that you think. Human beings can alter their lives by altering their attitudes of mind.

It is never too late to do this. One of the most successful and useful methods to help identify and clarify your thinking habits is by means of cognitive therapy.

Cognitive therapy

Cognitive therapy is the most heavily researched form of psychotherapy and has an impressive record in changing maladaptive patterns of thinking. It focuses on changing dysfunctional thoughts, emotions and behaviour. Above all, it teaches the power of thought: if you want to change an outcome in your life, listen to your thoughts. The aim is to teach us to identify automatic thoughts that are negative or distorted, to weed them out and to generate positive ones. For example, we make ourselves feel helpless because we are thinking, 'I'll never be able to do that.' We sabotage ourselves along the way by our thinking, focusing on the worst, fearing the worst, analysing and criticising and judging ourselves and others instead of experiencing the effects of positive thinking, of being in the here and the now and enjoying life's mysteries and wonderful experiences. Our limits are imposed through our belief in them. The aristocrat and garden designer Vita Sackville-West, who lived to the age of 70, once said, 'I worshipped dead men for their strength, forgetting that I myself have strength.'

We avoid important things by thinking: 'It can't be that important: I'll deal with it another time' (i.e. never). Or we may use withdrawal: 'The reason she hasn't called is that she doesn't like me so I'll keep right out of her way.' Cognitive therapy helps us to recognise those habits which are based on faulty reasoning. These are 'all-or-nothing' thinking, overgeneralising, and ignoring the evidence. We learn about our underlying cognitive structures, the templates we use to interpret information and which we assume are cast in stone but which are merely inherited and learned and which can be un-learned. We can be helped to modify them where they present problems. Cognitive therapy can be taught by a trained therapist or self-taught through multimedia learning programmes on the Internet (see Resources, page 202).

The therapy is focused on the 'here and now' and aims to develop rational alternatives. The resulting behavioural gains weed out ingrained negative attitudes and substitute new, fresh and positive ones. This makes a huge transformation in how we view the world and how we react to it. It makes it possible to set new goals, and to develop our mental fitness and functioning. It can open up our awareness in what can seem a miraculous way. Combining this retraining with good nutrition (see Vital Health Checks, pages 137–47) and physical exercise (pages 119–36), we can transform our daily living well into old age. So, 'Why not seize the pleasure at once?' asks Jane Austen. 'How often is happiness destroyed by preparation, foolish preparation.' Start today.

choices,
choices

choices, choices

Where nothing is sure, everything is possible Margaret Drabble

To work or not to work?

I believe in hard work. It keeps the wrinkles out of the mind and spirit. It helps to keep a woman going Helena Rubenstein

Whatever your age, there is great dignity in making a contribution to society, through your family, your community, or your work. However, to be forcibly marginalised in the world of work can be both de-energising and demoralising. Studies indicate that women whose work is rewarding deal better with the menopause, indicating that a career of some sort is good for your health. Trends towards mixed patterns of employment, earlier retirement, and increasing longevity, mean that we may enjoy many years of active work after what may in fact turn out to be our 'first' career, or even one of several. Whether you choose *not* to work any longer, or to embark

on a new career in your mid-50s, statistics show that you are likely to live for a further 35 years. With choices to make about work, further education, family, leisure and voluntary activities over this extended lifetime, we do well to prepare and plan it for ourselves.

With no compulsory retirement age in the USA (indeed it is illegal for businesses or professions to stipulate one), citizens may draw part of their pension yet continue in paid employment until the age of 67 when entitlement to full pension comes into effect. Similar legislation is being mooted in the UK and in Sweden. This goes some way to creating an ageless society, where the opportunity to work is not withdrawn because of a number – and in the case of women, five years earlier than men. However, shifting work patterns show that people are choosing to take voluntary retirement younger and embarking on new careers in order to fulfil a dream or meet a fresh challenge. Some people may be very happy to retire and stop,

feeling that work is not the preferred option; others may have years of fulfilment ahead of them in a new area of work.

As Aeschylus wrote in the *Oresteia*, 'The poet's grace, the singer's fire/Grow with his years'. Many of us are at the height of our powers in maturity. To continue in paid employment takes pressure off the pension system as well as improving our self-esteem: 'Grey hair is a crown of glory,' goes the biblical proverb. Society can gain many benefits from valuing people for what they bring and what they can do regardless of age. Understanding, knowledge, patience, wisdom, maturity and detachment are useful commodities in the workplace (which is not to say that *all* older people possess *all* these qualities).

In the late 20th century unprecedented changes took place in the consciousness of women, and in their place in society. None the less, accomplished women continue to be regarded as an anomaly. It is still common to begrudge a woman who has the gifts of intellect and intelligence, even more so if she happens to be attractive or even (no!) beautiful. Feminine charm, it seems to those whose thinking has not kept up with the times, must preclude other kinds of excellence. It is up to us not to put up with such nonsense.

Not only has what women can *do* changed, what women *mind* has changed. They mind still being the second sex. Working women in most places still earn only one half to three quarters of what a man may earn in the same job. Women are still a minority by most criteria except the numerical. At one extreme, there are women in small towns in central Italy, where cultural expectations still limit their choices, making fresh pasta twice a day for their men and ironing everything in sight including the sheets, not necessarily from choice. At the other end of the spectrum there are no-nonsense women voicing perfectly reasonable demands to walk the path of self-fulfilment and to contribute equally to society alongside men. This voice is increasingly to be heard in the over-50s age group as these women mature into their power, determined to make the most of the freedom of the empty-nest years.

Some pathfinders

I think leaders should encourage the next generation not just to follow, but to overtake Anita Roddick

'New women' are not without precedent. Even in past eras when men had the most power and influence because of their access to institutions, the wisdom and talent of women broke through: Catherine of Siena chose the path of the mystic, predominantly inhabited by males. Christine de Pisan wrote poetry in the late 14th century when poetry was the domain of men. Queen Elizabeth I of England defied the accepted archetypes of her era, not least by remaining single. Catherine de Medici (1519-89) and Madame de Maintenon

(1635-1719), both powerful women in the patriarchal world of a king's court, broke through contemporary prejudices and pursued their goals regardless of opinion.

In spite of not being allowed into the prestigious Academy of Science on the grounds of her gender, Marie Curie won the Nobel Prize for physics, the first woman ever to do so. She then went on to win a second, just to prove that it was not a fluke. Emmeline Pankhurst, arrested outside Buckingham Palace demanding suffrage for women after the First World War, said that she looked upon herself as a prisoner of war. She won that war. Josephine Baker (1906-75) broke all the rules about female independence (or lack of), refusing to recognise stereotypes of what coloured women could be, and proving her point by walking down the Champs Elysées in Paris with a leopard to demonstrate that black is beautiful. Jane Austen, George Eliot and then Emily Dickinson took serious writing to new places, and Dorothy Parker, satirical loose cannon with a sharp literary mind, wrote, 'I don't care what's written about me so long as it isn't true.' Martha Graham created a revolution in dance, retiring as a dancer herself at 76. 'It's not my job to look beautiful,' she declared, 'it's my job to look interesting.' She explored through body movement the spiritual and emotional essences of humanity and died at the great age of 96 having ripped apart many of the accepted dance conventions of the time.

Amelia Earhart represented the spirit of the American dream when she flew solo over the Atlantic in 1932. 'Women must try to do things as men have tried,' she said; '...courage is the price that life exacts for granting peace.' She accepted her aviation medal 'on behalf of all women'. Dorothy Hodgkin became a distinguished crystallographer and worked on the structure of penicillin during the Second World War. In 1964 she won the Nobel Prize for her discoveries in the structure of molecules, penicillin, vitamin B12 and insulin. Indira Gandhi, Golda Meir and Margaret Thatcher have all demonstrated to 20th-century society that women can be potent politicians, and the example of the eminent politician Barbara Castle is inspiring. Anita Roddick at the Body Shop, Barbara Cassani at Go airline, and Marjorie Scardino at the Pearson group, have all made groundbreaking changes in the face of business. In the world of the arts Yoko Ono and Rebecca Horn have broken new creative ground over long and distinguished careers. Georgia O'Keeffe challenged notions of style, theory and possibility in painting. An independent spirit, she said, 'I stripped away what I had been taught – to accept as true my own thinking.' She died at 98.

Jane Goodall, born in 1934, has made breakthrough discoveries in the world of chimpanzees, and says, 'We have a choice to use the gift of our life to make the world a better place – or not to bother... If you work hard enough, take advantage of every opportunity, and never give up, you will find a way.' Shirley Muldowney, the record-breaking racing driver, would surely agree: 'If you want something bad enough there are ways to do it. But you've got to stand your ground – if not they will walk over you like an old shoe,' says the 'queen of speeds', still racing at the age of 57. These women and countless others like them, many now into substantial old age, have blazed the trail for women everywhere, encouraging us to follow our star, and not to assess the odds but just to get out there and do it. None has been more inspiring than Germaine Greer, well known for her broadcasting, lecturing and writing as well as for her forthright views on many subjects furthering the cause for women's causes. She is one of the great women of the 20th and 21st centuries. Rich in intelligence, humour and personality, she has given many women much to be grateful for with her outspoken and often pioneering spirit.

Encouraged by the achievements, spirit and vision of these role models, as well as by many others, we can – all of us who want to continue contributing our gifts – find valuable ways of self-fulfilment through work well into our later years. In fact, we will be doing the community a service and it is vital for society that we do so, otherwise the young and ever-diminishing workforce (a result of the drop in birth rate) will have to look after a growing number of older people who become increasingly dependent on it. We can make a difference, each one of us, with our valuable contributions whether it is to family, to the local community, or to society at large either at a practical level or through the creative arts and education.

Diversity or discrimination?

Old and ready to learn is always young Aeschylus

If you have a vision, age is no barrier. There is no absolute biological or economic basis for giving up work at any particular age. Indeed, in agricultural communities most older men and women continue to work in farm production until they are physically unable to do so, which is often well into old age. In developed societies there is increasing recognition that people should be allowed to work as long as they wish, and older people at work, whether paid or unpaid, make a significant contribution to the economic prosperity of their country.

Age diversity is about getting the best person for the job regardless of their years. But the greatest obstacle to this path is age-discrimination. As far back as 1967 the US government passed a federal Age Discrimination in Employment Act, and similar legislation obtains in Canada and New Zealand. The UK still operates only voluntary codes of practice and it was only in the year 2000 that legislation was proposed if these were not followed. Meanwhile ageism is rampant and the people who experience the most prejudice on grounds of their age are in the 50-65 bracket.

In 1999 a yoga teacher made headlines in the UK when she was sacked at the age of 82 because her employers discovered that she was too old to be insured by them. She had been a qualified instructor for 32 years and her classes were full. She had 14 great-grandchildren at the time and looked and felt decades younger than her biological age. She was forced to abandon her four classes a week at the local leisure centre. If a person is capable of doing their job and doing it well, why should age be an issue?

According to a UK government survey carried out in 2000, 77 per cent of the general population felt that discrimination on the grounds of age was a waste of resources, but 78 per cent of the 50-64 age group felt that age was against them both at work and when looking for work. A similar percentage felt that their age was the principle obstacle to employment. The organisation Employers' Forum on Age, co-ordinated by Age Concern (see Resources, page 202), supports employers and encourages them to gain the benefits of an age-diverse workforce. Age diversity has been found to be in an employer's own interests, yet it has been shown that basing decisions on age can reduce their choice of a suitable candidate by up to a quarter. To the surprise of many, old dogs can learn new tricks: in her late 40s, my Russian friend Olga learned fluent English and Italian, emigrated to Canada, and educated herself in IT skills to a professional level. She found a good job and settled into a new life with her young son.

We can change the prevailing pattern – one person at a time. If each of us personally insists on articulating against age discrimination, and we define ourselves by our skills, abilities and potential, we can show the world that age is irrelevant.

A creative cocktail

Sooner or later I'm going to die, but I'm not going to retire
Margaret Mead

A famous slogan during the First World War read, 'Your country needs you!' The new women of the early 21st century could well sport the same logo. Society cannot afford *not* to employ us: businesses are being encouraged to come up with more flexible work environments in which older people can serve as consultants and mentors, a policy that could benefit the clients as much as the employees.

A shorter working week of 20 hours could be ideal for employee and business alike, making it feasible to employ able people even into their 70s, whether on a part-time basis, or job-sharing with a young colleague, which gives them a chance to share knowledge and experience. Businesses that have started to do this have found that employing people over 50 is a worthwhile investment: they are the most reliable age group, more prompt, more conscientious, more experienced and they tend to get on better with customers and colleagues. It is unwise to write off whole swathes of the population who have well-honed skills and a sense of history to pass on. In an age of transformation from a manufacturing to a knowledge-based economy, this age group is a critically under-used resource. In a world where almost nobody has a job for life, using the talents

of older people makes for a more balanced community life and better inter-generational understanding.

A culture of part-work and consultancy, part-retirement, part-voluntary work is a healthy mixture for the individual and society alike. It is a creative cocktail. If we view this new scenario as one of welcome balance, as opportunity rather than as a catastrophic problem we can more easily highlight the possibilities that can open up for older women. But it is up to us to seize these opportunities and take an active part in history in the making. The prospects are after all more delightful than sitting at home with not enough to do and feeling worse and worse about ourselves and about life. Society needs us, so it's up to us to get out there and show the world what skills and energy we have. Let us challenge the concept of retirement, keep on updating our options and enjoy the combination of work, volunteering and leisure pursuits in this wonderful era of our lives.

'If you don't risk anything,' wrote Erica Jong, 'you risk even more.' It is our responsibility to revolutionise 'retirement age', and since many of us are not ready for indulging in a 'third-age sabbatical' this is less of a problem than it might seem. Although retirement *can* mean a comfortable relaxing time to indulge in leisure pursuits, this is probably more often a dream than a reality. Retirement may be a cruelly abrupt change in lifestyle, which can mean financial insecurity, loss of structure, boredom, subsequent depression, and loss of the

companionship of the workplace. In short, loss of citizenship. We have positive choices to make and it is up to us to choose.

What are the choices?

It takes as much energy to wish as it does to plan
Eleanor Roosevelt

The choices are: to change course completely in your career; to decide to stay in your job, but insist on making the changes you require to improve your situation; to work out a 'creative cocktail' (page 44); to look at doing voluntary work; to teach yourself IT skills; to return to or start academic studies; or after long service in employment, to put all your energy into enjoying family life and being a fulfilled grandparent. Whatever your choice, be inspired by Lauren Bacall's remark 'I am not a has been, I am a will be.'

A Change of Career

At whatever age, a change of career is not easy. But with courage, determination and a goal in view, everything is possible. Take that leap into the unknown (the net usually appears!)

Action is the antidote to despair Joan Baez

How to go about it

My success was not based so much on any great intelligence but on great common sense

Helen Gurley-Brown

First of all, decide on the area in which you would like to embark on a new career, whether it is using people skills, your creativity, entrepreneurial abilities or organisational skills, your knowledge, your time or your assets. If communication skills are your strong point, for example, if you are good at networking and you like the idea of working from home, you could consider becoming a head-hunter.

- You can use **knowledge and experience** to become a trainer, lecturer, teacher or coach, medical receptionist, accountant or bookkeeper, or to branch out into new fields of business and industry.
- Using **specialist skills**, you could set up a new business, take up selling, secretarial work, word-processing or editing, horticulture, painting and decorating, dressmaking, translation or interpreting, floristry, cooking and catering, home help, counselling, security work or housekeeping.
- If you have **assets** why not look at training to be a teacher, becoming a landlady, taxi-driver, going into desk-top publishing, taking up market-gardening.
- You can offer your **time** in jobs like care-

taking, prison work, being a warden or club steward, an administrator, market research interviewing or house-sitting, teacher's aide, school manager, local councillor, magistrate, manning helplines.
- If you are looking for **ways back in**, take a look at becoming a housing officer for a housing association, a clerical assistant to a professional body, a social work assistant, or nursing auxiliary.
- If you want to test your **creative skills**, look at photography, graphics, gardening and garden design, website design, interiors, writing, or creative house decoration.

Then

- Look in job centres, employment agencies, newspapers and journals for ideas and vacancies.
- Open your mind and explore even the most unlikely ideas.
- Acquire new skills as well as a new mindset. Take a risk!
- Start networking early. Get to know other people in other fields.
- Get out of large corporations if you work in one: become independent.
- Decide whether or not to seek vocational guidance. Some 'human resources' consultants may charge you a lot of money to tell you what you can easily find out for yourself on the Internet or in the library.
- Check out useful learning environments such as: adult learners' centres; colleges; libraries;

nurseries; local radio; schools; TV; universities; arts centres; businesses; museums and galleries; nature reserves; newspapers and magazines; sports centres; the Internet; book shops; churches; homeless shelters; national and local parks.

- Check out any social benefits and allowances that you may be eligible for from the state while you are searching.
- Check out free computer courses for job-seekers.
- If you are starting a new business, check out local training facilities (see Resources, page 202) that may provide information, advice and skills training for new businesses.
- Look out for organisations (see Resources, page 202) that find part-time expenses-only jobs for people with professional experience.
- Find workshops to help you to realise the value of your experience and knowledge (see Resources, page 202).
- Present yourself positively, as a set of skills rather than as a veteran!
- Don't allow yourself to think that you won't be 'good enough' because of lack of training or education. Anna Freud (1895-1982) said that 'creative minds have always been known to survive any kind of bad training'.
- Check out your employment, financial and holiday rights before signing new contracts.

Working Out a Creative Cocktail

To create a new balance between work, family and voluntary work, see page 44.

Voluntary Work

One thing I learned the hard way was that it doesn't pay to get discouraged. Keeping busy and making optimism a way of life can restore your faith in yourself Lucille Ball

Working in this sector may offer you an opportunity to enhance your self-esteem at the same time as helping others, and give you a sense of value within the community. Voluntary work provides social contact and a platform for learning skills, and this in turn may even lead to paid employment as you engage in your chosen field. This may be the Red Cross, the Blue Cross (working with neglected animals), Amnesty International, Citizens' Advice, Oxfam or other international charities, or helping people in day care centres. Driving, cooking, administrative and people skills can all be put to good use. There is a huge demand for listening skills on helplines, which could trigger an interest in training in more specific counselling skills. Patience, a good heart and liking people are sterling qualities – if you have them, give them!

Details about work in these areas and many others can be found in your local library, such as adult literacy; equal opportunities organisations; housing and accommodation; disabled; action and information services; out-of-school care; agriculture and food; AIDS and HIV; alcohol and drug addiction; animal welfare; arts and crafts;

driving services; benevolent associations; bereavement; media and broadcasting; business and industry; care for the elderly; local hospital; children's health; helping children to read; counselling (Relate, Samaritans, Cruse etc.); Citizens' Advice Bureau; education and training; emergency relief and international aid; environment; ethnic minorities; health and medicine; human rights; law and justice; learning disabilities; museums; mental health and illness; peace organisations; recreation and leisure; rescue services; sports and exercise; VSO; women's organisations; women's health; youth services; zoos.

IT Skills

By the year 2000, nearly 10 million people over the age of 55 were using the Internet (83 per cent of them logging on daily). This figure makes up a quarter of that age group and one fifth of the total number of users. This just goes to prove that you are never too old to learn: in fact a computer is as important to their lifestyle as it is for those in their teens and 20s.

If you are not one of this number, don't succumb to technophobia: the learning curve is not that steep, so don't be intimidated. Basic computer skills are not rocket science; they are easily acquired and a lot of fun, rather like playing with a new toy. Talk to a friend or someone you know who has some experience, and get them to show you the basics, and to help you out when you get stuck. Computer technology –

whether you're exploring websites, finding information, communicating by email, visiting chatrooms, or researching your favourite areas of interest from politics to poetry, the environment to spiritual matters – can be a productive leisure activity as well as a way of sourcing information for many areas of life. Just typing the key word on your search-engine (Altavista, Metacrawler, Google etc.) home page will bring up a wealth of possibilities and links: it's as simple as that. Financial services websites are extremely popular with the over-50s age group as they can cut many corners and reduce costs in your planning (see Money Matters, page 170). Email is a beautifully instant yet quiet and non-invasive means of communication to anywhere in the world and a wonderful way of keeping in close touch with friends and family at almost no cost.

The UK government has launched an 'IT for All' initiative that offers tuition and training, computer 'tasting sessions' and Internet demonstrations to encourage the tentative. There are numerous on-line tutorials (see Resources, page 203) that give practical guidance on major Internet topics ranging from basic to advanced, teaching how to use software, tools such as email and shopping on-line, and even designing your own web pages. Mobile IT training sessions piloted by Microsoft with Age Concern will soon become widely available.

This is the technology of here and now, and of the future. If you get left behind you will be marginalised, and you will miss out. It's a lot of fun. Enjoy the ride and being part of the initiation

of change, recognising the key experience of keeping the mind active, the spirit positive and finding enrichment through the myriad opportunities made available by the Internet.

Lifelong Learning

In youth we learn; in age we understand Marie Ebner-Eschenbach,

Education does not end with school or even college. Our early schooling plants seeds that can flourish in maturity. Learning later in life enhances your *joie de vivre*, improves your self-confidence and decreases social polarisation based on age. We all have untapped potential: discover your hidden abilities and ignite dormant passions. Broaden your horizons and embrace new subjects. Nearly 50 per cent of baby-boomers participate in adult education: never has there been a wider range of subjects on offer at evening classes, via distance learning, or at degree level. One of the greatest privileges of being alive at the beginning of the 21st century is that the opportunity for adult education is so widely available and accessible to most income groups. You can join evening classes, you can take a mature degree, and you can do much in between these two levels.

Some options
Courses in computers, languages, aquamobility, art, martial arts, upholstery, theatre studies, yoga, counselling, most subjects at GCSE and A levels, psychology, keep fit, history, cookery, pottery, relationship skills, chess, music, needlecraft, woodwork, anthropology, car maintenance, stained glass, creative writing, garden design, textiles, dance, massage, philosophy, line dancing, photography, sculpture, religious studies, silk painting, sugar craft, local history, homeopathy, starting your own business, economics and current affairs, literature, science, engineering, classics, environment, health and social care, humanities, law, popular culture, and much more.

There are many different types of qualification and places to study including:

- local evening classes/community education
- post-graduate university degree
- diploma or certificate in higher education
- Open University
- distance learning courses
- University of the Third Age
- Open College for the Arts
- University of Industry
- learning on-line

Local outlets
Adult education courses are widely available, run by local authorities. Details can be found in your local library or by contacting the authority by phone. Subjects range from astronomy and badminton to yoga and Zen meditation.

Universities and colleges
Many universities run extra-curricular courses,

which will qualify you for a diploma or certificate in higher education. Certain colleges accept mature students for degree courses. Colleges of Further Education offer community education courses for older students.

Schools

Some schools take in mature students, studying alongside the younger pupils. Many are interested in promoting intergenerational activities and understanding.

Special interest groups

Local community clubs, societies, museums and other organisations including religious ones run special interest groups. Check your local library for information.

Libraries

Use your library for much more than just borrowing books: it is a mine of information on local and national activities, it provides Internet access and sometimes open learning centres where you can learn to use computers. CDs, CD-ROMs, talking books, cassettes, reference books and much else are on offer.

Personal learning projects

For the independent-minded who prefer to work on their own, you can use the library extensively for research too. Learning how to use catalogues, microfiches and directories efficiently and fluently is a great help. The Internet is a goldmine for research, for almost any topic under the sun. A good search-engine will start you off on your journey through cyberspace, where you will come across all kinds of unexpected treasures. Audio-visual resources are available too, and most libraries have an efficient inter-lending system for books they do not carry on their own shelves. You can tape TV educational programmes and use their back-up material. The BBC (see Resources, page 202) produces a free catalogue of all language learning programmes.

CD-ROMs are a rich resource for self-education. Linguaphone run complete courses on CD-ROM in many languages, and you can teach yourself anything from equestrian skills to family trees. Encyclopaedias, dictionaries, the complete *National Geographic* magazines, a tour of the world's great museums, and travel companions are available. You can build up your vocabulary with the help of a CD-ROM, learn history, do crosswords, organise your money and your tax, do quizzes, and go to 'mind-gym' – all in the comfort and safety of your own home!

Distance learning

Open learning or 'distance learning' means studying at home with a tutor who is geographically distant but usually available on email and accessible for tutorials. Day schools are often included in this formula. The Open University (see Resources, page 203) runs a wide range of degree and other courses. Find out details through your local library, the Internet, or local newspapers and magazines.

Details of the organisations mentioned above can be found in the phone book, on the Internet (Age Concern, for example, have a useful site), and in reference books (see Resources, page 202).

Family and the Community

For the sake of making a living never forget to live anon.

The place of the older woman at the heart of the family has always been of central importance in society. Nothing is more vital and creative than the stability, understanding and love that a mother and grandmother can provide for her immediate relatives. She is our most important teacher and role model. This job, although unpaid and often unsung, is probably the most taxing yet worthwhile that a woman can do. Many women make the family, with all its pitfalls and difficulties, their life's work, and there will surely never be a time when the qualities of patience, kindness and loyalty become redundant.

With the family at the heart of a healthy society, the woman's role has a wider social implication than simply to her immediate loved ones. The effect that she can have on the development of human relationships is frighteningly powerful, and the skills required are not necessarily instinctive: they may have to be learned (see Love Is All There Is, page 72).

Being an active grandparent is a demanding but rewarding task, which has fun as well as pain built into it. If you have no grandchildren and wish you had, you could consider becoming a surrogate granny; there is a Foster-Grandparents Organisation (see Resources, page 203) that offers this opportunity. Because grandparenting is not (usually) a full-time job, it provides spare time in which to do the things you never had time for previously, and to achieve the kind of work-life balance that most of us would aspire to.

For many women, this time of life opens up opportunities for working in the community and doing public service work like representing the local community on the parish council or helping out in the local school. Carers also play a huge part in oiling the wheels of the community. With exceptional compassion, kindness and commitment they do the essential work of looking after the mentally and physically disabled, the old and the sick, putting up with huge stress, long hours and low pay. It is impossible to put a price tag on this work: in fact the potential financial value of caring done by older people is equivalent to more than the total expenditure of the whole of the personal social services in the UK! This underpaid – often unpaid – work is shamefully undervalued. Society (not to mention the chancellor of the exchequer) is indebted to these unsung heroines (and heroes), and their invisibility is by no means a reflection of their worth. The value of this work within family and community is of core importance not only to the individuals concerned but also to society in general.

brain power

brain power

*Think wrongly, if you
please, but in all cases
think for yourself* Doris Lessing

Use it or lose it

Your mind is your best definition of YOU. Growing old happens in the mind.

Doris Lessing is right because the better use you make of your mind, the less you are at the mercy of the outside world. How you look after your mind in later years is just as important as how you look after your body. Your brain is the most beautiful bit you've got (and very likely your biggest erogenous zone too).

Mental agility is an important pathway across the map of successful ageing. The brain is a muscle, and for optimum performance, just like any other muscle, it needs exercise, rest and the right nutrients. It gets better as it matures – if it is looked after in the right way. So make the most of it; if you don't use it you lose it. The harder you use it the more it grows, just as your quadriceps muscle grows when you do rowing or running training. Brain cells, if they are not used, actually die of boredom: they atrophy if not stimulated.

The brain weighs the equivalent of a bag of sugar, about 1.6kg (2lb). It accounts for 2.5 per cent of your total body weight and up to 20 per cent of your body's energy needs. The quantity of nerve cells inside your skull as you read this equals approximately the number of stars in the Milky Way – about 100 billion. Every nerve cell or neurone, each one of which has a branch system known as dendrites, is capable of being connected to up to 100,000 others by means of a synapse, and each of these synapses involves at least 50 different chemical transmitters. The interconnections between them can form patterns and memory traces that amount to a numerical infinity (6.5 million miles of 11-point typewritten zeros!).

Your brain can improve with age if it is used well. Its potential is huge, yet most of us under-use

Attitude is all: do you see this as half full or half empty?

it dreadfully (some scientists suggest that we use only 1 per cent of its capacity). The more interesting the challenges you give to it, the more synaptic connections are made and the more it can evolve. Not only that, brain cells physically improve their powers of association and so the more you learn, the easier it becomes to learn more. Back in the 1960s Dr Tim Bliss observed that cells change at a molecular level when they learn something. By taking mental and physical exercise into our later years we can keep our wits sharp and our reactions lively.

Brain cells – and here is the key – do not connect and grow of their own accord. They need help.

- Mental stimulation is the essential nutrient for the growth and complexity of brain cells. It has been shown that synaptic connections can be physically improved by proper exercise of the brain. Increase your thinking apparatus by giving it constant challenges and problems to solve.
- Take adequate exercise (see Vital Health Checks, p119). A quarter of the blood in the body is used by the brain, therefore any exercise will help to nourish it, because of the increased blood flow due to cardiovascular activity.
- Eat a healthy diet (see see Vital Health Checks, p137). The brain burns glucose and oxygen at ten times the rate of all other body tissues at rest. Carbohydrates and oxygen are the two most important nutrients for the brain.
- Take B and E vitamins which are good for brain function.

- Don't drink to excess: alcohol activates glutamates which stimulate your neurotransmitters, thus enhancing cognitive function, motor control and learning, but – and it's a big but – *too much* alcohol deactivates this process.
- Chronic stress and high anxiety levels release cortisol into the bloodstream and this 'cooks' your brain cells! Learn to relax and bring balance into your life.
- Non-conformity keeps your brain cells stimulated – that is, not behaving in the way that you think you 'should' behave, or even as you think other people should behave. Enjoy being true to yourself.
- Don't smoke (see page 118).

The mind-body connection

Physical Exercise

Human beings move around. In common with the rest of the animal world we are animated, as opposed to plants which do not need brains like ours because they are rooted to the spot. We need our brains to be in full working order to maintain our connection to life. Our animation is an integral part of our consciousness, and command-control is lodged in the brain. Virtually all communication relies on movement of some kind, however minimal. Movement is life.

The movement of gentle exercise increases the

Take up a new challenge.

efficiency with which oxygen is transported around the body. By improving blood flow to the brain and endocrine system, the growth of new brain cell 'branches' or dendrites, down which, simplistically, thoughts travel, is increased. The effects of exercise protect the body from the deleterious 'stress response' where, under chronic excessive stress, so much cortisol is released into the bloodstream over time that it destroys brain cells. Exercise burns off stress hormones and stimulates the secretion of noradrenaline, the stimulating brain chemical or neurotransmitter that improves mood. The release of endorphins into the bloodstream relieves depression, with the result that exercise can sometimes be a more effective therapy than a talking cure.

Too much exercise however is as ineffective as too little (see page 123). Follow the guidelines for exercise in Vital Health Checks (page 119) making it as enjoyable as possible so that it becomes a welcome break from other activities in your day.

Mental Exercise

Take up a mind-sport:

- chess
- bridge
- quiz games etc.
- crosswords
- travel
- new adventures
- learn a language
- study a new subject

- take up painting
- become/stay socially involved
- remain open-minded and flexible in your thinking

Taking up physical and mental exercise may involve changing your habits. If changing habits seems difficult, think of it this way:

Habits are not prison walls although they may feel like them.

- An old habit is only a memory-trace in the brain, an established synaptic connection.
- A new habit is a *fresh* memory trace that can become as established as the old one in under three weeks.

The body-mind

A healthy brain is important not only for mental function but for emotional well-being too. Everything is connected. Our moods are chemical reactions resulting from a series of events or a single trigger. If serotonin for example is released in the brain in response to a pleasurable experience, you feel happy. If something stresses you, the stress hormones adrenaline or cortisol are released into the bloodstream, producing either a fight-or-flight reaction or a longer-term series of symptoms such as sleeplessness or irritability. We are walking cocktails, and the cocktail shaker of this chemistry is inside our skulls.

What you think, therefore, affects your brain activity, which in turn affects your mood or emotional state. If you think gloomy thoughts,

Old habits can be replaced by fresh new ones.

you feel down; if you think positive thoughts, you feel bright. You can control your feelings by controlling your thinking. All too often negative thoughts come from wrong perceptions anyway: 'She doesn't like me', 'He's cross with me', 'They don't care', 'It's never going to work out' rattle through our minds when actually the reverse may be true. In such cases our negativity comes from within ourselves and not from other people: we've got ourselves into a twist just by thinking the wrong thoughts about the situation.

What it comes down to is that the endocrine system, which produces our happy or sad hormones, interfaces with the brain. Mind meets body here, thought meets feeling. When we understand better what our mind-body connection is and how it operates, we can have more control over it. By controlling our thinking, we make positive steps towards the balance that is intrinsic to good health. Thinking in a particular way is a *habit*, and we can change our habits (see above).

The optimists versus the pessimists

I have a quotation stuck over my desk, which is remarked on by everyone who sees it: 'In the middle of difficulty lies opportunity.' Einstein said that (his brain had 400 per cent more glial cells than average: they are the ones that aid interconnectivity in the brain circuits). In essence, an optimist can be defined as someone who sees opportunity in difficulty, a pessimist one who sees difficulty in opportunity. The latter, according to medical research, is a life-threatening condition because long-term studies have shown that pessimists are more prone to illness and die younger, on average, than optimists. Optimists weather coronary bypass surgery better, and live longer with HIV, according to the *Journal of Personality and Social Psychology* (1998). People who remain optimistic in the face of powerful stresses have more killer cell activity in their immune system, whereas pessimists' levels don't change. Your thoughts and feelings affect your immune system: the more optimistic you are, the stronger your immune system, and the less likely you are to become ill. The relatively new science of psycho-neuro-immunology (PNI) has come up with startling results in this field and concludes that our minds can really make us ill: negative thinking can affect our susceptibility to real, physical diseases by directly influencing the immune defences, to which our thoughts are connected via electrical and chemical communications pathways.

Up to a point we are all intrinsically 'situational' pessimists or optimists: you tend to believe that the worst will happen, or you see the best in most situations. We appear to be wired up that way. The good news for pessimists, however, is that there is ample evidence to suggest that they can reprogramme themselves to become more optimistic. Cognitive therapy (see page 35), which encourages people to identify and change habitually negative thoughts, has excellent results

in this area, and is one of the most useful ways to help us retrain the way in which we think, in order to change our habits for the better. Like any other aspect of our health, it is up to us to make choices and take steps to prevent ourselves from becoming habitually negative.

Some people find that, as they age, they acquire the habit of complaining or of focusing on the gloomy side of life. However, this pattern is *not* an inevitable part of the process of ageing. Most of us encounter suffering and difficulty during our lives. Some people deal with this well, pick up the pieces and go forward, others allow life's burdens to hang around their necks like an albatross. We may not even be aware of how negative we are becoming as we grow older. Statistics show that pessimists are usually to be found in the older age group so we will be doing ourselves a favour if we take a close look at ourselves to see if this is happening. It could be life-enhancing not only for us but also for those around us to weed out the possibility before it becomes an entrenched habit.

Help is at hand: for cognitive therapy, see pages 35 and 202.

You are what you learn

If you rest, you rust Helen Hayes

What you learn and read and remember over your lifetime contributes hugely to the person you are. We see in people who lose their memory the tragic consequence of loss of identity. 'She's not my mother any more,' a friend said sadly about her ageing parent with Alzheimer's who no longer recognised her and remembered little of her own past. My friend kept up her visits until her mother's death, but it was a harrowing experience for her to watch her mother's decay. The terrifying fact is that Alzheimer's disease and other forms of dementia affect 50 per cent of those who live to 85. It is the third highest cause of death by disease in the USA after coronary heart disease and cancer. The only good news about this is that it can be delayed – even prevented – by proper 'brain-care'. Although the jury is still out, it is believed by some doctors (see Resources, page 203) that long-term mental stimulation may play a part in warding off, if not preventing, dementia, although our genes may well play the greater part. It's worth a try, anyhow, and at the same time it makes life more interesting. While we still have our minds intact, we are blessed. The more we make of our minds, the richer we become as people, whether we choose to develop spiritually, intellectually or both.

As society moves into the information age of the 21st century, into a 'knowledge economy' based on brain power, we will probably have to work quite hard to keep up. It's fashionable to say that the facelift of the future is a neural upgrade. Well thank heavens for that, it's a whole lot better than the other sort. We can count our blessings. By keeping our personal wits in good order (which is a good deal more genuine and less painful than cosmetic surgery), we are less likely to be marginalised in older age. There is no need to fear: the brain can get better and better as we get older. We do, after all, come with more experience, more individuality, more (one hopes) wisdom, and a huge bank balance of several decades of life history. It is up to us to harvest these and make the most of them.

Many of us, as we move into the – hitherto relatively uncharted – territory of life after 50, have more opportunities to explore new directions than did women of previous generations. We are better educated – or if we are not, we have a chance to become so with the availability of lifelong learning at our fingertips either on the Internet or through local classes (see pages 53-5). We may be empty-nesters tasting freedom for the first time in years, or choosing a change in our work lives that gives us time to take up new challenges. These wonderful opportunities enable us to make a valuable contribution to the new knowledge economy with the blend of maturity and experience that we can contribute.

Expanding horizons and starting to explore new directions is the opportunity of this time of life. It is a prescription for good brain health. The sociologist Karl Mannheim said that we need to cultivate 'perfectly universal minds enjoying an elasticity such as to make it possible at any time to start afresh'. This may be a point in our lives at which we can benefit from one of the many advantages of maturity – the erosion of narcissism. Instead of being obsessed with whether people like, admire or are impressed by us, we can begin to let go of that. Just small things – taking risks in conversation, expressing our own opinions with conviction and standing our ground without caring about what others think, or making our own jokes instead of laughing at others' – take us in that direction. Live dangerously! It will stimulate your brain (and in any case, it's better to burn out than rust out in my opinion...). Your potential is greater than you think.

It is never too late to start learning. All of life can be a learning experience if we allow our brains to be challenged, thereby building brain activity. It may be travel that stimulates and broadens your mind, or study, or spiritual practices, or learning to play chess, but whatever it is, go for it.

Education is an ornament in prosperity and a refuge in adversity. It is the best provision for old age. Educated men and women are as much superior to the uneducated as the living are to the dead Aristotle

Memory fitness

Had a senior moment recently? Walked into the next room to get something but couldn't remember what it was when you got there? Forgotten a name yet again? Lost the car keys? Or is negotiating maps a constant problem? (Don't worry, this is something that actually improves

Making Memory Maps

Once you understand that your memory works by imagery and association, you can apply these techniques to everyday life whether in business, at home or just to clarify your own thinking. And it's fun. Using pictures, numbers, arrows and other connective devices, and making use of colour too, you can map out whatever it is you are working with (a business plan, a synopsis, taking notes in a lecture, or your Christmas list). All you need is paper and felt-tips (or just a pen or pencil – add the colour later when you have more time).

Start your map at the centre of the page. Make a branch system from this centre as you go along, adding more branches as you go out towards the edges of the page, in different directions, employing images and numbers wherever you can. Select key words which stand alone and which connect to the central image. Add in colour at the time or later. You will find that the image of this page will be recalled by your memory far more easily and clearly than a simple written page or a list. It's simple and it's brilliant – try it!

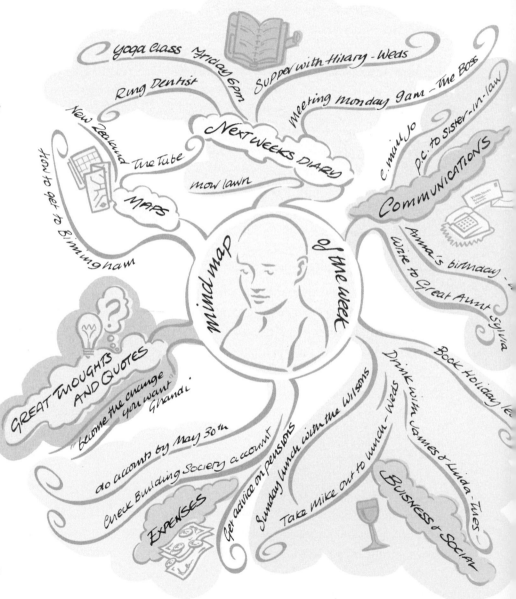

Yoga class Friday 6pm
Ring Dentist
Supper with Hilary - Weds
Meeting Monday 9am - The Boss
New Zealand
The Tube
How to get to Birmingham
MAPS
mow lawn
Next weeks Diary
e-mail Jo
P.c. to sister-in-law
COMMUNICATIONS
Anna's birthday
Write to Great Aunt Sylvia
mind map of the week
GREAT THOUGHTS AND QUOTES
"become the change you want" Ghandi
do accounts by May 30th
Check Building Society account
EXPENSES
Get advice on pensions
Sunday lunch with the Wilsons
Take Mike out to lunch - Weds
Drink with James & Linda - Tues
Book Holiday le
BUSINESS & SOCIAL

after menopause! Recent research shows that these particular spatial skills thrive on less oestrogen.) If you accept these 'failings' as a fact of life, a fact of ageing, you're wrong.

We are our memories, and to a great extent our survival as 'whole' beings is dependent on them. If you constantly forget the details of things that connect people to you in relationships, or where you left the car, what day it is or your own address, you become disconnected from those around you. Not only that, memory is also rich with meaning and associations and is integral to a full life experience. Nutrition and exercise play an inevitable and important part (see pages 114–39), but specific to a 'neural upgrade' is the exercising and training of the memory.

Training your memory is a form of aerobics for the mind and it becomes more vital the more the years tick by. If it doesn't motivate you nothing will – and motivation is a key factor here. (Actually it's intrinsic to the notion of genius, a genius being a person who will treat the whole of life as one gigantic test to puzzle out, and will relish all the challenges thrown at them. And according to the geniuses themselves, it's more about sweat and toil and hard work than anything else. Geniuses we may not be, but their example is inspiring.) Without motivation, we are unfocused and unable to concentrate our energies effectively; we may become cynical and nihilistic. Cynicism is the enemy of growth.

There are various ways of training the memory. Crosswords, chess and bridge are excellent brain-stimulators (see page 62), but mastering a simple mnemonic system can help us to realise that we can control and modify our own mental processes.

The 'memory men' of ancient Greece taught the concept of linking the thing you want to remember to a familiar place, a striking image, or a rhyme. This is still the fundamental thinking behind all modern systems of mnemonics. The key to a good memory is the ordered arrangements of the objects to be remembered. This can be achieved by using particular props or mnemonic techniques.

- A rhyme ('Thirty days hath September, April June and November' etc.).
- Principles of association: making a powerful image in your mind: when you meet a man called Jonathan (David and Jonathan/David and Goliath). Or remember his green shirt and hook the name to the shirt in your mind...
- Memory-mapping (see alongside).
- Speed-reading: time yourself reading a page. Then read it again using a pointer to help you focus, and, always moving forwards and never back-tracking, begin to take in two words at a time instead of one.
- Keep socially involved: it is shown that degeneration of memory occurs faster in people who lack regular contact with others.
- Keep your brain active: learn a new subject or a language; read, listen, do crosswords and other mind-games.
- Oestrogen levels seem to affect memory function, and it has been shown that post-

menopausal women on HRT function better than those with low oestrogen levels.

Give your head a treat

Your mind can benefit as much from physical treats as from mental nourishment. Yoga and meditation bring calm and balance, and increase clarity and insight. The following treatments are also beneficial.

- Indian head massage or 'champissage' is excellent therapy for the head. It can help to correct disrupted sleep patterns, induce relaxation, relieve tension headaches, eye strain and migraine, and reduce hair loss resulting from stress.
- Aromatherapy using lemon balm (*Melissa officinalis*) in a base oil is calming and sedative, and has also been shown to help people with moderate to severe dementia. This essential oil is thought to interact with the brain pathways that are affected by Alzheimer's. You can also use it in the bath or in a burner.
- A daily capsule of the herbal remedy *Gingko biloba* (see Resources, page 203) is known to improve concentration significantly, and taken together with ginseng has a powerful effect on cognitive improvement, with faster reaction times and better memory function.
- Cranio-sacral therapy, which involves a light hands-on treatment lying on a couch, balances the spinal fluid and has many beneficial effects, as does acupuncture.

A simple guide to meditation

Meditation changes brain wave activity, inducing theta waves which have powerful effects on brain function as well as on bodily health. Meditation is good for:

- learning ability
- lowering biological age
- creative problem solving
- hearing and vision
- blood pressure
- heart disease and cancer
- stress
- drug dependency (including alcohol and nicotine)

1 Set aside 10–20 minutes once or twice a day.
2 Choose a quiet place where you will not be interrupted.
3 Sit comfortably, either on a chair or on the floor. Stay upright but relaxed, with your eyes down (or closed). Relax your face and smile a little. Place your left hand palm up in your right hand, on your lap. Breathe normally, feeling the movement of the breath in the body.
4 Follow your breath not your thoughts, creating a distance between the activity of the mind and the process of breathing. Think of thoughts as a movie projected on to a screen in front of you: you do not *have* to watch the movie!
5 If you find this difficult, count the breath: count 1, breathe in, breathe out, count 2, breathe in, breathe out and so on until you get to 10. If you wander off somewhere before 10, return to 1.
6 Alternatively, use a mantra, a favourite word or phrase that appeals to you, which is positive and peaceful.
7 When you find yourself distracted by the antics of the monkey-mind, gently turn back to focusing on the breathing or the mantra, without self-criticism and judgement, because that kind of reaction is just what the mind feeds on!
8 Sit quietly for several moments after your meditation comes to an end, enjoying the silence and stillness, before moving back into 'real' life.

love is
all there is

love is all there is

*That Love is all there is
Is all we know of Love* Emily Dickinson

Knowing yourself

Your relationship with yourself is probably the most important relationship you'll have in your whole life. The better you know yourself, warts and all (without, that is, beating yourself up constantly about your failings) the more chance there is that you will have healthy relationships with other people. If you are honest about your own faults you are more likely to have a sense of humour, to be compassionate about others' shortcomings, and be able to relate to them more openly. Some people seem to be quite comfortable in their own skins, and appear to know themselves well, instinctively, while others find it harder to discern truth from illusion. However, if too much introspection can lead to unhealthy self-obsession, the refusal to accept what we are really like can be destructive to those around us, as well as ourselves in the long run. So, task number one in the whole subject of love, as philosophers and poets from many cultures tell us, is to get to know yourself.

The latest research shows that what matters more to older people, more than anything else, is relationships. Relationships need care and attention as well as selection. We need to make clear choices about discarding destructive relationships gracefully, and nurturing positive ones. Neglecting the challenge of managing our interpersonal relationships can lead to negativity, loneliness, boredom and self-pity.

You are more likely to make worthwhile and lasting relationships if you have some degree of self-knowledge and can be honest with yourself. Most relationships are, to some extent, founded on projections: everyone we meet mirrors something in ourselves and shows it back to us. We risk disappointment and disillusion if we fail to recognise this. The bits we see in other people are the only things we *can* see, because they relate to something inside ourselves. If we know about ourselves and take responsibility for our own material we are less likely to make unwise

projections and end up being crushed by statues.

The concept of 'self-altruism' may at first sight appear self-indulgent, but if you follow it through to its conclusion you can see how it can have deeply compassionate effects. If you are kind to yourself, you are more likely to be kind to other people, not least because both feel so pleasant! Kindness is a habit, and we are in control of our habits (see page 63). Looking after your own emotional well-being equips you with the tools to develop friendship skills and to find richness in positive relationships because whatever you put into them is returned, unasked, with interest. Being loving means that you will be loved. At the outer level, but corresponding to the inner, 'the smile that you give out comes back to you' (this is a traditional Indian saying). It's worth trying, even when you don't feel like it. Smiling usually works.

The way in which we approach self-knowledge and self-altruism as individuals is as varied as we are individual. In essence, the path is an inner path. Without these qualities, the spiritual decay of 'old' sets in: no spiritual decay, no 'old age'. In the words of W. B. Yeats, age is 'paltry...unless soul clap its hands and sing'.

Some Keys to Mature Self-Altruism

- Humour.
- Letting go of the illusions of youth (omnipotence, immortality, perfection).
- Realising that everything is not about YOU: life is about itself.

- Taking responsibility for your own life and growth and development.
- Realising that you can think, feel, say, decide and do what you want so long as it doesn't harm others.
- Understanding that blaming others is not only weak, it's useless.
- Having an honest relationship with yourself.
- Developing new relationships with others, especially friendships.
- Opening up to change (this may be your last chance).
- Developing new forms of creativity.
- Embracing a more reflective and less materialistic way of life.
- Not engaging in a desperate struggle to retain youth's beauty. You'll never win, and in any case age has its special beauty.

Does 'Self-Knowledge' Mean Going into Psychotherapy?

Not necessarily. There are pros and cons. You could end up with a severe case of umbilical whiplash and spend your 90s grumbling about the deficiencies of your potty training. Bear in mind that there is no evidence that any one of Freud's patients was actually cured of their neuroses. His writings are highly regarded as a form of great literature and can be usefully viewed in this light.

The word 'psychotherapy' means, literally, healing the soul. But many of the analytical schools of therapy are more about tightening the manacles of the mind than healing anybody's soul. When it comes to throwing light on self-knowledge, analysis risks influencing people according to its own concepts and models of the world rather than allowing them to be themselves. Patients can often become so busy accumulating this information, and being introspective, that they become perpetual students to a task-master. There's not much room for compassion in this exchange. Analytical therapy has confused knowledge with understanding, and substituted this knowledge for experience. It promotes a culture of judgement and blame. In the broader field of psychotherapy you may have more luck with cognitive and object-related therapies than with analytical ones.

By all means study psychology in order to understand more about your psyche, but bear in mind that psychology does not go the whole way to explaining the human predicament. It may reveal, but it does not cure. It is limited, and some therapists are more limited than others. A brilliant therapist can give you brilliant insights, but a dim one can simply confuse you and waste your money. The great 19th-century Zen poet Ryokan wrote:

Mind itself is the mind
That leads the mind astray
When you ride the mind-horse
Never loosen the reins!

There are several brands of analysis that give you a sense of being absolved from all responsibility, and that flatter the ever-hungry human sense of self-importance. Personally I have learned more about my psyche and dealing with difficulties through practising a simple form of Zen meditation, reading literature and watching drama, than through the mind-games of analytical psychotherapy. Many of its traditions ignore the more intense and profound depths of the psyche that can be stirred through religion or meditation or great art or great music – healers of the soul all.

Analytical psychotherapy was the new religion of the 20th century (the main difference being that therapists charge for their work where the Church does not) and has largely run its course. Analysis was the modernist answer to the established Church, producing its own dogmas, with high priests who were sometimes no less corrupt than their sometimes less-than-celibate counterparts in orders. There are good and bad practitioners of course, but for the latter sin, blame and guilt were and are the focus of their skills, and many is the victim of this approach. Analysis digs up guilt, anger, fear, pain, resentment – all of which we have to face and deal with and integrate in our lives. But focusing on them can make us vulnerable to manipulation and dependence on the so-called expert, the therapist. The transference that can occur between analyst and client can lead many people into further confusion and certainly makes them lighter in the wallet. Inadequate therapy can throw dark shadows of blame and judgement over the lives of the client. It may lure them into the trap of masochism and self-sabotage. The most important question, therefore, to ask yourself before you go down the therapy route is, am I the protagonist of my own life, or a victim of my circumstances?

None of this is fair on the good therapist or priest who works with compassion and understanding to provide their client with tools to feel happier about their lives. I know some really good ones. It's just that there are many ineffectual therapists who end up abusing the vulnerability of people in pain. Woody Allen, after 40 years of therapy several times a week, said he didn't think it had done him any good. Yes, the talking cure is as old as the hills and can be truly valuable, a lifeline: cognitive therapy (see page 35) is excellent, and marriage guidance invaluable, but it's not a good idea to pay someone to supply answers for you about your life, personality and destiny. It's best to find them out for yourself. And the profoundest of these insights are as likely to be found in great literature, poetry, music and drama as they are in a discipline that purports an authority it cannot possibly possess. 'Why have analysis when you can read?' asks Adam Phillips in his book of remarkable essays, *Promises Promises*.

How Does 'Soul Clap its Hands'?

Everyone will find a different answer to this question. Generally speaking, soul flourishes more easily in some places than others: it is less likely to do so in a shopping mall or in front of the TV than in a quiet spot of your choosing. Here are some basic suggestions:

- being outside with nature
- learning to view the world with an almost childlike sense of wonder
- practising regular meditation
- following a spiritual discipline
- being creative
- being in touch with others' creativity
- studying the great thinkers, poets, musicians and wise men and women
- learning to be alone and happy in solitude
- working with and for other people

Several international research projects have shown that involvement in some spiritual path or religion – active participation rather than just a belief – has positive effects on your health, prevents illness and delays death. The importance of community and fellowship, the psychodynamic of ritual and the underlying optimism of many spiritual paths appears to be good medicine for body as well as soul. Positive intention (and this can include prayer) can be better therapy than excessive introspection.

Involvement with any of the suggestions listed above tends to take us out of ourselves and our more petty preoccupations into wider ways of being, thinking and feeling. Great enthusiasm may ensue – that wonderful word for passionate eagerness which derives from the ancient Greek meaning 'being possessed by a god'. We are refreshed by this. 'Without worship we shrink,' wrote Peter Shaffer in his play *Equus*, whether that worship be formalised or simply experiencing the awe of nature as we look at a tree in full autumn colour. That is one choice of many that we are free to make at any age. 'There is no path in the sky; the monk must find his inner path,' said the Buddha, and this time of our lives is a great time to unlock the door to the interior life and let the soul sing.

> *The wisest men follow their*
> *own direction*
> *And listen to no prophet*
> *guiding them.*
> *None but the fools believe*
> *in oracles,*
> *Forsaking their own judgement.*
> *Those who know,*
> *Know that such men can*
> *only come to grief.*
>
> Euripedes

Balancing solitude and sociability

Eleanor Roosevelt said that 'the purpose of life, after all, is to live it, to taste experience to the utmost, to reach out eagerly and without fear for newer and richer experience.' That can be as true of the exterior world as of the interior, and a balance between the two brings rich rewards for most people, although I remember a very down-to-earth farmer saying to me, when I was talking

about the blissfulness of stillness in meditation and yoga, 'Don't go along with that myself. After all, you're a long time dead.' But then you can be dead to the immensities of living, too, by not touching your own depths of creativity and feeling and imagination and soul.

Meditation can act as a mirror reflecting the solution to our problems, achieved passively rather than actively. It is a powerful tool and a wonderful physician. Here we can find joy in the present, and beauty in things that transcend desire. We experience the great commonplace that the best time of life is always now. We rest not in torpor but in the happy ceasing of fretting and getting. We slow the pace, and instead of accelerating into craving and anguish we experience the joy that is always available in the here and now. We learn to trust life. (For meditation techniques, see page 71.)

Time on our own can give us the space to touch on the wisdom available in great literature, drama, poetry and music, all of which belong at the heart of spirituality. Since our lives are created and defined by our thinking, it is useful to take inspiration and counsel from greater souls than our own. Having been a bookworm and music addict in my youth, but distracted by other avenues of life in my middle years, I am now rediscovering these riches even in the midst of a busy working life, and am aware that if I don't read and listen now, I may run out of time. The pleasures are enormous. It is not just learning what other people already know, nor is it about getting answers to the big questions. It's more about understanding that the unknowable is unknowable, being content with that uncertainty and enjoying the richness of the mystery.

'Pleasure lies in being, not becoming', wrote St Thomas Aquinas. This is something that for many women becomes clearer with age and maturity, and one of the great gifts of meditation is that it helps us to be still and access that mode of being. We take this quality of serenity out of the meditation space into the hurly-burly of the world where it stands us in good stead. Krishnamurti said, 'if you could walk alone among these hills or in the woods or along the long, white, bleached sands, in that solitude you would know what meditation is ...The ecstasy of solitude comes when you are not frightened to be alone.'

Solitude can be liberty, it can be a great teacher, it can bring deep contentment (in the right doses), and each of us needs to find the levels that suit our personality. As a 50 per cent introvert/extrovert, I find that a 50-50 balance suits my temperament well, and an imbalance stresses me. It's worth doing a personality test (see Resources, page 203) to explore which ratio might suit you so that you can balance your inner-directed needs with your outer-directed ones. Inner-directed needs focus on individuality, non-conformity (a healthy option according to medical research!), finding out about yourself, and personal fulfilment. Outer-directed needs are more about wanting to be part of a group, to conform and to be liked. Both are valuable, and we can weigh up the scales evenly, for us as individuals, by spending some time alone, and some time working for and with others with whom we are so closely interconnected. As the proverb goes:

Every one and each are brothers
None goes his way alone
What we put into the lives
of others
Comes back into our own

Friendship and love

The Greeks had six words for love. We have only one. This is not particularly helpful. There are shades and degrees of 'love', which often overlap, and that are useful to define in order to clarify our personal relationships:

- agape – charity or selfless love
- ludus – playful friendship and love
- sorge – the close companionship of sibling love and friendship
- pragma – the long-established love of partners
- eros – erotic sexual chemistry
- mania – infatuation and obsession

The definition of friendship in the "Shorter Oxford English Dictionary" goes 'one joined to another in mutual benevolence and intimacy ... not ordinarily used of lovers or relatives [this is an interesting distinction!] ... One who wishes another well ... Anything helpful.'

'I always feel that the great high privilege, relief and comfort of friendship was that one had to explain nothing,' said Kathleen Mansfield (1888-1923), and Marlene Dietrich likewise defines friendship as essentially unconditional: 'It's the friends you can call up at 4 am that matter,' she said. We do well if we keep old friendships in good repair, and nurture new ones throughout our lives.

Probably more words have been written in literature, poetry and song on the subject of love than any other. Divine love, human love, love of life remain the most potent of forces to determine human behaviour along with its opposite, war, with which, as two sides of a coin, it is inextricably linked. It is hard to avoid clichés on the subject of love after everything has been said about it, so let a cool dictionary definition suffice: 'that state of feeling with regard to a person which arises from recognition of attractive qualities, from sympathy, or from natural ties, and manifests itself in warm affection and attachment'. Further descriptions include 'strong predilection for or devotion to (something)...the affection between lover and sweetheart...and instance of being in love...the sexual instinct and its gratification...a beloved person...to entertain a great regard for...to hold dear...to embrace affectionately'.

For many women, as they mature, love has less to do with need than it did in youth, and is less narcissistic. There is less fear, jealousy and pain in a late-flowering love relationship, more deep bliss, more quiet happiness and peace, more tenderness and appreciation of the specialness of love than in the hot-headed and perhaps future-oriented

Staying lively longer means we can enjoy the younger generations more than ever.

attachments of our more self-centred youth. We realise that, in the words of Sarah Bernhardt, 'it is by spending oneself that one becomes rich', rather than by assuming protection, gratification or advancement through love. 'We can only learn to love by loving,' wrote Iris Murdoch, and since love has much to do with forgiveness we can forgive ourselves our past 'mistakes' by seeing them as part of a valuable life lesson.

The Chinese say that it is difficult for love to last long, and that one who loves passionately is cured of love. Not everyone would agree: perhaps that is true of a love based on collusive narcissism. But however painful or disillusioning a failed love relationship might be, the human heart is renewed with joy when love touches it. The key to not being disillusioned is to stay with the feelings of love and pain and not to allow the mind to stray into the realms of craving. Wishing things to be other than they are, projecting into a desired future, can despoil the mysterious miracle that can light up our lives so unexpectedly and inexplicably, however late in life.

Camus wrote that 'in the midst of winter I finally learned that there was an invincible summer'. Here the tired soul and the shrivelled heart recover their energy and fullness in love, youthfulness returns to the bloodstream, and life is richer in every moment. Love is potent magic, and to remain open to it in later years, in whichever form we meet it, enriches our souls. Love of our grandchildren may ignite it, or deepening love for our children, the love that manifests in friendship, the love of a lover, the love of nature, the love of our fellow creatures, the love of a beloved animal, the love of the divine, the love of music or of learning; all these loves energise us and make us happier, making those around us happier too.

The latest research in a study of the over-90s indicates that they regard not death as their most important preoccupation, but the forming of new relationships, and 13.6 per cent reported a new relationship every year. And why not? Good wines improve with age, and the finest wines taste the best when well matured.

Other relationships

A recent survey showed that in terms of relationship satisfaction, married men come out top, single women second, and (way behind) at the bottom, married women. Partners aside, the dominant relationships in our lives as we turn 50 are often with our kids. Mothers and grandmothers of this generation are often closer to their children than was the case in the past. There is less of a generation gap because we feel healthier and livelier at this stage of life than our predecessors did, we have more opportunities to keep on learning, we stay younger longer. We are more likely to be able to communicate effectively with them, and engage in their world with open minds. As they move away from home or even go abroad, we now have the gift of email. Keeping in touch in cyberspace is wonderful. It is immediate and informal, and you can 'chat' far more easily than you might in a letter, and you are likely to do so more often simply because it is such a simple medium. The phone is, as it has always been, a great means of contact too.

We also have the chance to rejuvenate neglected relationships which might have suffered while we were busy working or bringing up a family. This can apply as much to friendships as it can to our partners: empty-nesters frequently need to rediscover each other in the space now left to them.

The older we become, the more importance family may assume for us. However, family relationships are often a minefield. We all need courses in how not to be the mother-in-law from hell, the intrusive mum, the know-it-all grandmother, the daughter-in-law smelling of burning martyr or the vengeful sister. We have no training for these life skills and often the example of others is not always that useful. To learn how to clear up the mistakes of the past, the misunderstandings and the quarrels, we can be helped by the self-knowledge that is such a useful acquisition at this time of our lives. Who needs the unfinished business of broken relationships hanging around their neck? Redeeming them frees us to move forward into more positive ground in many areas of our lives. It is incredibly liberating. For terrific insights into close relationships and family bonds, you can do no better than read *Life and How to Survive It*, and *Families and How to Survive Them* by John Cleese and Robyn Skinner. It's all in there.

Some of us may encounter care-giving responsibilities as our parents and grandparents live longer. This is too big a subject to cover in the limitations of space here, and too important to be dismissed in a few paragraphs. However, there are some excellent websites on the Internet (see Resources, page 202).

Now that one in three marriages in the West ends in divorce, more and more people live alone. How do we develop that central relationship with ourselves in the context of this single existence? If you have never lived alone, how can you do so happily? How different is it to living with a partner?

Some advantages of the single life

What a lovely surprise to discover how unlonely being alone can be Ellen Bursten

Whether you choose to be single or whether the single estate is forced on you by circumstance, counting the blessings of the single existence can be a useful exercise. After my friend Pauline's husband died suddenly of a heart attack in his late 40s she was left stunned with grief, with two teenage children to support, to cope on her own after two decades of a happy marriage. She will never 'get over' her loss, she will always love the man who shared her life and her children, but she

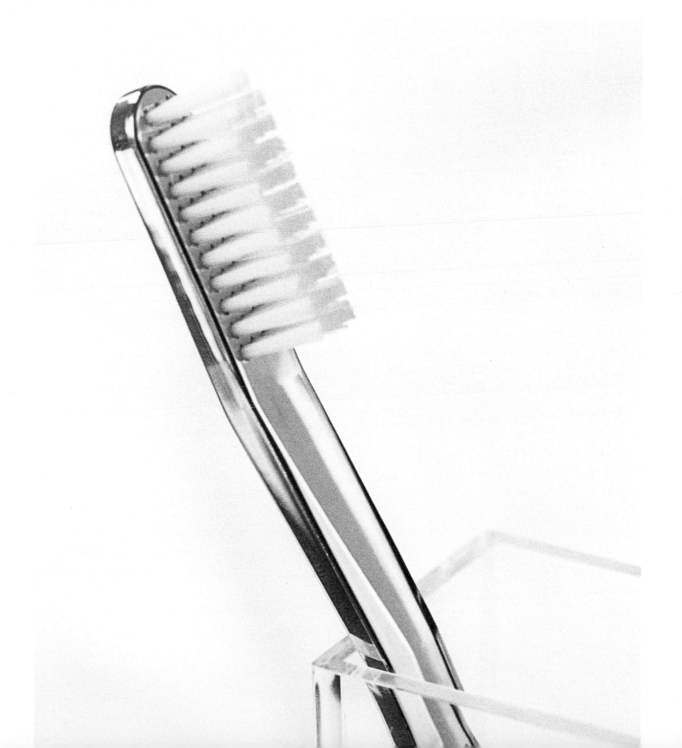

has come to terms with her enforced single existence with great courage. She sailed across the world twice crewing for (all-male!) racing yachts, threw herself into voluntary work, joined a yoga class, and moved from a small isolated village into the local town. All of these were 'firsts' for her. She also wrote copiously to express her feelings, a useful safety valve if not a lifeline, and has maintained a busy social life.

After a catastrophic end to her marriage culminating in acrimonious divorce, Tessa decided to go and live in London where she could indulge her passion for theatre and for a while she worked as a PA for a small company. Then she took up working for the mentally handicapped, and devoted much time and energy to seeing her sons through college. She resolutely looked at the positive side of life, and is one of the funniest of my friends, a delight to be with and an example of courage over the odds. She packed her bags for the Sydney Olympics and disappeared to the Southern hemisphere for six months simply because she'd never been there. Her emails from the Barrier Reef said it all...

Cath has never married. She lives close to her mother and sister and works full time in education, lecturing and freelance teaching. She lives simply and contentedly, according to her values. She enjoys her solitude, the countryside around her where she walks her dogs, her independence, being able to follow her own body-clock and work to routines that enable her creatively. She has a wide scope of interests and is always interesting to talk to, valuing friendship as one of life's greatest joys. These three women are inspiring examples of people who make the most of living on their own.

Perhaps at some level we all recognise the choice between 'single thraldom or double strife' (Francis Bacon's aphorism on whether or not to marry). 'I don't need a man to rectify my existence. The most profound relationship we'll ever have is the one with ourselves,' was the view of the author Katherine Mansfield. Her words are worth recalling in moments of doubt when social norms overwhelm our better judgement and we contemplate chucking in the single towel for some dream of bonded bliss. It is equally worth remembering that the triumph of hope over experience does not always have a happy outcome.

- Some relationships come with sell-by dates. They may become toxic after that time.
- Other people's relationships often look better from the outside than they actually are: if you could be a fly on the wall...
- Other people are *not* always having a lovely time at weekends and Christmas. More than likely they are wishing devoutly to change places with you!
- Even if you have been the loser in a relationship, there will have been valuable life-lessons in it.
- If you have lost a dearly beloved partner, you have treasured memories (and some people are not so lucky).

- The freedom of living alone and leading your own life can be fantastic.
- Your independence can be a thing of great value, difficult though it may be sometimes.
- You can establish life routines that suit you such as eating and sleeping whenever you like.
- You could get a dog or a cat as your team mate.
- You are free to spread your wings and do things you have never done before.
- You can move on, and grow.

The art of living alone

When my own marriage ended in a spectacularly unpleasant way in 1984 – my *annus horribilis* – I was forced into living alone in a state of pain and anger, confusion and misery. It was a long struggle working my way through the dark times – it was a great life crisis! – but after a while I began to stop looking back, and to relish what life had handed me. 'The manure of experience,' I muttered through gritted teeth. I threw myself into my work, started doing courses, took up yoga and eventually became a teacher, and discovered friendship. I discovered also the comfort and healing in relationships with animals. The lifelines that these at first represented became, eventually, resources of great depth and creativity that would define my way of living. Looking back now, I am grateful for what happened to me, something I would originally have thought impossible. How can you be grateful for open-heart surgery without anaesthetic? Perhaps because without it I would have died. I had the chance to go in another direction, not of my choosing at the time, but which now, in retrospect, I would choose again. Along the way I evolved some strategies for living alone (you probably have your own to add to this list).

- Keep your friendships in good repair.
- Plan. Forward-planning is important when you're single; it gives a structure to your life.
- Learn to initiate, however shy you may feel about asking people to do things with you, or joining in a group.
- Keep busy, but allow enough time to enjoy being on your own.
- Develop new friendships with people of all types and ages.
- Build up a solid support network of plumber, builder, electrician, DIY man etc. so that you don't feel isolated in moments of practical crisis.
- Keep a pet: dogs can be the most unconditional of friends, and cats are wonderful too.
- Eat regularly and well, and not too much or too little (see Vital Health Checks, page 137).
- Take regular exercise – it keeps your spirits up.
- Rearrange your bedroom to be the room you always dreamed of.
- Have people to stay from time to time – but never for too long, otherwise friendship is put to the test. 'Superior people never make long visits,' said the American poet Marianne Moore (1887-1972), wisely.

Sex and love

Cultural taboos around discussing the sex lives of people over 50 die hard. Lovemaking for wrinklies is perceived by all except those involved to be vaguely disgusting. But interiorly, so to speak, people do not perceive themselves as old as they may look. Figures show that seven out of eight couples at 50 have sex with each other, at 60 seven out of ten, and at 65 it's 50 per cent. But the media do not portray older women as sexual beings, or even as desirable: usually great screen lovers are well under 40 (with the possible exception of Charlotte Rampling who embodies a free spirit, a subversive and passionate agent of her own destiny. But this is far from the norm in representation, however much closer it may be to what actually happens in real life).

If, as a younger woman, you were perceived as a sexual object, it is your prerogative in maturity to turn this around and become the protagonist, and make the running for a change. By changing the emphasis to tenderness and feeling rather than looking and desiring, you can create the possibility of the most contented and fulfilled sex life you have had for years. If you want to. And in whatever way you want to. You may well *not* want to in which case you can make clear choices between the alternatives (see page 91).

The influential ideas of Freud and Havelock Ellis have permeated thinking around sexual behaviour for nearly a century, instilling the notion that penetrative sex represents health and happiness. Perhaps it was in their interests to do

so. It is received opinion in some quarters that sex is obligatory, even as we get older. After several decades of a sex life some women would not agree. Many have lost interest; they are frankly bored with it – their 'conjugal rights' repetitive and even repulsive. And there are, of course, large numbers of older women who have never married, who are divorced, or who are widowed – indeed about half the population of women over 50 do not have a male partner. Of those who do, not all have a particularly active or exciting sex life for a variety of reasons. As Alex Comfort puts it so memorably in *The Joy of Sex*: 'The things that stop you having sex with age are exactly the same as those that stop you riding a bicycle – bad health, thinking it looks silly, no bicycle.' He could have added 'boredom'.

But lack of sex is only a problem if it's causing a problem, and for most women the problem will be more about a warm and loving relationship than about sex per se. If that has dwindled, the sex will die, but if it is rekindled by new eroticism, desire can blaze just as ferociously as it ever did in the younger body. This may happen in a rekindled love between two longstanding partners, or it may be triggered by a new relationship. The strong feelings created around this latter resurgence, however, need to be carefully contained: they may not represent a deep and lasting love. They account partly for the culture of serial monogamy in Western society, which is so costly in terms of emotional and mental suffering. This kind of love may not always flourish under domestic tedium, it may be more about 'ludus' and 'eros' than 'pragma' (see page 81).

The Alternatives

Lifelong sex is one of the great myths of the 20th century. In fact, you might be persuaded to think that it is mandatory. As the journalist Julie Birchill put it, 'There has probably never been a time in history when women knew so much about sex and wanted so little of it' (*Guardian*, 6 March 1999). A 1999 study, a Kinsey Report for the American Medical Association, found that 40 per cent of women have no interest in sex compared with 8 per cent of men. Many of these women take the view that there is love without lust. The disparity, though, means that impossible pressures come to bear on partnerships unless they are recognised and met. Do 'conjugal rights' flaunt human rights of women? If so, are there not alternatives to coitus which maintain intimacy and satisfaction, sensual alternatives of physical closeness predicated on a less erotic form of love for the other? Surely. Even holding hands can be one of life's most sensual and rewarding emotional experiences. The arm around the body, the light kiss on the lips, the stroking that expresses simple tenderness and affection, can be infinitely more satisfying than full-on sex. One of the sensible things that Freud said, perhaps only stating the blindingly obvious, is that all a human being needs to be happy is love and work. Sex is only an also-ran in this line-up, especially for women, because for a lot of women sex doesn't really work: orgasm is not the inevitable outcome as it usually is for men. As women become more enlightened and confident they feel more able to reject sex as a necessary part of the pattern of relationship, not just because of its failure to deliver but also to step outside the power-struggle that is intrinsic to its tyranny. It is rare that love between two human beings exceeds need, and the needs awoken by sexual activity can become monsters that can undermine the love. To break the circuit and step outside this ring of fire, to acknowledge the disparity of desire and need that can cause such resentment and frustration in a partnership, requires skills built on mutual love and understanding. Exploring gentler sensual pleasures is a route that can work for many of us.

As we age, the basic truth about attraction becomes clearer as narcissism diminishes: this is that our brains are our largest erogenous zone. What really takes place between two people is a mind-exchange, its outward and visible manifestation being the physical relationship. When the latter gets into difficulty, it is worth looking at the former and doing something to stimulate it. Sharing interests makes powerful bonds. Creating new joint activities can lead to adventures and surprises that connect you together in new ways. Diversifying your approach to physical intimacy as a result can be deeply satisfying: cuddling, kissing, hugging, mutual masturbation and oral sex can become more

pleasurable than the penetration routine which, as men age, becomes more tiresome for them too. They have fewer erections (and they are less strong), there is more difficulty in ejaculation, and the whole performance can become a tedious nightmare.

Why tolerate bad sex? Added to which, intercourse may become painful for post-menopausal women (see page 164). Sex does not have to be all about penetration and orgasm, not all the time. There's more to it than that. Read love poetry to each other naked, by candlelight. Try it, it's highly erotic. Inventing your own aphrodisiacs, while keeping the physical/sexual threshold low, can be incredibly arousing. It's surprising how many couples use sex-toys, too, in their later years: they are long past feeling shy with each other and are open enough to make some of the running with new arousal games. The ease, familiarity and affection that instil the confidence of a long relationship are part of the delicious fruits of sex in later years.

Some women, for whom this is not possible on account of the nature of the relationship or the absence of one, will be perfectly happy to relinquish sex. They do not see the emancipation from the duty of the double bed as death-in-life. Far from it. It may be an important part of their freedom in the later years. It is not, as might be perceived from the outside, a disqualification because of the menopause (i.e. sex means procreation and therefore a fertile, younger body), but rather a fully conscious, happy decision to invest in a relationship of a different kind, and in a different way. Choosing celibacy can be immensely liberating. The tyranny of the sex power-struggle no longer holds sway, and new freedoms evolve around friendships and personal life. Celibacy can release energies that are often trapped inside life-models based on the inevitability of sexual behaviour. It becomes possible to be truly open-hearted without reserve, regardless of gender, as your own woman, when you are committed to your own celibacy.

For other women, the cultural divide of the menopause may release them to change sexual orientation and find great comfort and relief in a relationship with another woman. The energy and implicit understanding that can arise between two women can be, for some, a satisfying path in a new phase of their lives and an outlet for sexual hunger that may not be satisfied in a heterosexual relationship where, in some cases, male potency is on the wane. Menopause can be the beginning of new sexual awareness, whatever form it may take.

Masturbation may be this form. As long ago as the 1940s a Kinsey report found that half of widowed, separated and divorced women in their 50s masturbated to orgasm on average every three weeks, and that one third of women masturbated within marriage. A Consumer's Union survey in the USA in the 1980s showed that over one third of women continued to masturbate into their 70s. This is the great unmentionable secret that still, in the so-called liberated days of the 21st century, induces feelings of guilt and embarrassment. But masturbation is an important release, a unique reliever of tension which is both pleasurable and harmless. It may unlock emotions of unhappiness, loneliness or grief for lack of a partner, which instead of being suppressed can be acknowledged and mourned, and therefore partly healed. It is an important ritual for pleasure, too, if you spoil yourself with aromatic oils and soft music and low lights. Enjoy it. It relaxes the body, and while promoting the deep rest that comes after orgasm, it energises and refreshes.

Lonely Hearts

One of the saddest documentaries made by independent British television in the late 1990s focused on some over-50s looking for love. Then, on a lonely hearts programme, *Blind Date*, early in 2000 three 80-year-olds (no less) made an appearance hoping to catch some bait to spice up their lives. All of these women filmed spent their time wishing that their lives were other than they were, even though they were full of blessings. They seemed unable to contemplate manlessness, and their strategy was to dress to kill in low-cut tops, bright colours, gaudy jewellery, high-heeled shoes, overdone make-up and short skirts. The synthetic sexuality that they exuded was so patently mutton dressed up as lamb that it seemed designed to evoke pity. Desperate for a man in their lives, they consulted dating agencies and newspaper advertisements, eager to find lasting romance (which of course is a contradiction in terms.) 'If you think you are finished, you are,' said one of them, expressing what appeared to be the totality of her philosophy of life. These were women who connect the fading of physical beauty with a man's lack of interest. To many women, this would speak volumes about the man and the nature of his desire, but for these women the catch, the romance, the dream was the only thing that mattered.

These women were stuck in the adolescent mode of thinking only of the effect of their body on the other, and missing the point about the freedom of no longer having to be the spectator of your own performance. That sex becomes, with maturity, no longer just the surface attraction of allure and beauty and arousal. They had failed to grasp the chance that age offers to be themselves. Had they done so, some nice blokes might have been queuing up for them. As it was, over the nine months of the filming of the documentary, none of them found a mate; they were all as unhappy and confused at the end of programme as they were at the beginning, searching for something that does not exist.

Generally, if you are looking for love it eludes you. It usually comes when you are looking the other way and hits like a meteor when you are not expecting it. A late spring of love often comes uninvited with the menopause: Catherine the Great was said to have had a climacteric that 'teased her like her teens'. Perennial fairy stories of the old hag transformed into the beautiful princess

bear witness to this. If love does strike like this, and you decide to risk the pain along with the joy, you need to be prepared on a physical level (nothing can ever prepare you on the emotional and psychological levels – that is part of the script that we cannot write).

Late-flowering Sex

It is assumed that the menopause disqualifies women from an interesting love life, but this need not be the case. Here are some tips and hints for a happy sex life over 50.

- Vaginal dryness is a common problem for women at and after menopause, due to the decline in oestrogen. But remember that vaginal cells never lose their ability to respond, and can be revived, either by the use of creams, or by arousal itself.
- Use over-the-counter lubricants if dryness is a recurrent problem; they make the mechanics of sex easier, but remember that good sex is about emotional connection. Don't use baby oil or massage oil because it can be irritating, and can also degrade condoms.
- Vitamin E oil can relieve itching and irritation, and counteracts dryness.
- Low-dose oestrogen creams are available to apply to the entrance around the vagina. You only need small amounts – usually less than is recommended by the manufacturer.
- A 'hormonal ring' is used by some women to keep up oestrogen levels.

- Remember that the best lubricant is desire and arousal. When the emotions and the psyche are happy you will probably find that there is lubrication aplenty.
- Learn some new foreplay techniques, or use sex toys.
- Turn the lights down low, use candlelight, burn an erotic oil like sandalwood or ylang-ylang in a vaporiser.
- Orgasm is not the be-all and end-all of sex, for either of you. Enjoy the tenderness and the play. Keep communicating. Talk about it.
- If you embark on a new sexual relationship, check your partner's sexual history. If you are at all uncertain, use a condom. It is a good idea to get tests done for any sexually transmitted diseases if you have failed to do so. Discuss this with your doctor.
- Keep your pelvic floor muscles toned with this exercise:

For a toned abdomen:

Contract the muscles that you use when you stop peeing mid-stream. It is as simple as that. You can do this at any time of the day, you can do it sitting, standing around, driving, anywhere. It makes a fantastic difference to the tone and shape of the lower abdomen. Less sag, more flatness. Brilliant. It works!

skilful beauty care

skilful beauty care

You can take no credit for being beautiful at 16. But if you are beautiful when you are 60, it will be your own soul's doing Marie Stopes

Mutton or lamb?

Coco Chanel was of the opinion that beauty (and she should know, it was her business) starts with the heart and soul. Without that, cosmetic care is a waste of time. The old adage that beauty is from within may be a cliché but it is so often true. Your individual beauty starts with your personality, but can also be enhanced by lifestyle (so you can always make the most of a bad job!) You can do much to help the radiance and energy that are intrinsic to natural beauty by eating well (see Vital Health Checks, page 137) and exercising regularly (see page 119). But while you can't radically change your assets, nor can you put the clock back despite what the advertisers would have you believe, you can make the most of your skin, hair, nails and feet the natural way.

Ivana Trump was reported as saying that 'Donald wants me to stay 28 so I told him it is going to cost a lot of money.' For what? Who is going to be deceived? Cosmetic surgery offers lip shaping and ear improvement and hair transplants and face lifts and nose reshaping and breast surgery and liposuction and laser skin resurfacing and eye bag removal and abdominal reduction ...The science of ageing is offering us designer drugs in the guise of the nectar of immortality. No thank you. This may appeal to some women but it sounds like a Faustian pact gone mad to me. It must be exhausting to spend your life pretending to be a girl by plastering over the so-called ravages of time and simulating the youthful body. Give me natural any day.

There are plenty of ways of giving nature a hand and I am all for that. When you let go of narcissism, says Doris Lessing, 'you realise that

what in fact you've been using to get attention has been what you look like… Growing older is extraordinarily interesting.' Looking after the ageing body, accepting its changes as an intrinsic process, can be deeply pleasurable and can also help you get the best from it.

Your personal style, your character, your intelligence and good spirits become your most important assets over 50. To coin a paraphrase, things inside grow as things outside go! The face, which cannot lie however thick the mask and however skilful the skin tucks, tells us (and the world) much about our lives and about ourselves. Those habitual frown lines, or corners of the mouth drawn down, say more than anything about our attitude to life.

Mutton dressed as lamb is abhorrent and never succeeded in its deception anyway. If you are happy and confident in yourself you can be far more convincingly glamorous: it's just in a different way than it was two or more decades ago! The face becomes something to be looked out of rather than to be looked at as an object of seduction (forget that). As Anita Roddick points out, 'it is your demeanour, the way you walk, the language you use. With age comes the humour and the laughter I did not have in my twenties'.

'Taking joy in life,' said the Hollywood star Rosalind Russell, 'is a woman's best cosmetic.' Beauty becomes about who you are, not what your mask looks like or whether you are following the latest dictates of fashion. The beauty of good health, tranquillity, graceful movement, and a sense of humour (nothing is more attractive than a genuine smile) outshine the most sophisticated of cosmetics. There can be mystery and intrigue in a lived-in face, and elegance in choosing the right colours to wear to suit fading skin and hair. If we look after our looks in a natural way, we can be confident in this new kind of beauty. As Emily Dickinson put it so gracefully, 'Beauty is not caused. It is.'

Natural skin care

As we age our skin becomes less elastic, and once we reach menopause it tends to become drier. Although the quality of our skin depends largely on our genes, there are lifestyle factors than can help to keep it relatively soft and supple, and certain natural oils that can be just as good, if not better, than some of the most expensive skin creams on the market.

Commonsense Tips: Dos and Don'ts
Do
- drink lots of water
- get out in the fresh air and take exercise
- wear sun-screen in the sunshine
- get enough restful sleep
- eat fresh organic food in order to avoid chemical pesticides and fertilisers
- meditate: it works wonders on relaxing the face
- keep your face clean, without using soaps or detergents which dry out the skin

- use creams with anti-oxidants to mop up the free radicals that pollute the skin
- drink green tea which contains anti-oxidants
- treat yourself to a moisturising mask from time to time (see below)
- use natural toners such as rose water or orange flower water, rather than products that contain alcohol which dehydrates your skin
- wear colours that lift your natural skin colour: the colours that used to look good may not any more: look at new colour schemes!
- apply to your neck whatever oils and creams you use on your face
- wear high collars or scarves to detract attention from the inevitable signs of ageing on the neck

Don't
- sunbathe: it puts 20 years on to your age, dehydrating and wrinkling your skin
- use a solarium: ditto
- allow yourself to become stressed for long periods
- drink too much caffeine or alcohol, both of which dry your skin out
- miss your sleep
- expose yourself to too much central heating or air-conditioning
- skip meals: repeated obsessive dieting adds a decade at least to your face
- smoke: your skin becomes grey, lined, pallid and tired-looking
- wipe creams off your face with abrasive cloths, which damage its fine texture, or cotton wool

which often leaves fibres in the pores. Use a soft, damp face cloth instead

Natural Oils for the Face
Most commercial skin creams are based on water, oil, wax, lanolin, alcohol (which you don't want since it dries out the skin) and glycerine – simple household ingredients. With little expertise you could go to the kitchen cupboard and save yourself time and money – and, possibly, the risk of being conned.

Simple plant oils nourish the skin and restore its suppleness. For best effect, put them on to the skin while it is still damp – after a bath or shower, especially in really dry places like knees and elbows. Apply your chosen oil with a soft cotton pad and allow it to soak in before wiping off gently with rose water.

Olive oil is one of nature's best lubricants. The original beauty creams of 2000 years ago were based on olive oil.

Hemp oil is wonderfully softening for very dry and sensitive skins.

Groundnut oil is particularly good for the dry skin on the neck.

Almond oil was used by the ancient Greeks to restore the skin's natural oils depleted by the hot sun. It is rich in vitamins and minerals. Good for wrinkles, as is apricot oil.

Coconut oil smells wonderful and is deeply enriching for ageing skin, especially around the eyes. Excellent for after-sun care too.

Avocado with honey makes a fabulous skin conditioner.

Jojoba oil is a highly protective oil which penetrates the skin well and nourishes it.

Wheatgerm oil is a light oil rich in vitamins E and A, which counteracts dryness. Just puncturing a capsule of a vitamin E pill and applying it to dry patches can be an instant fix!

Sesame oil is good for stretch marks.

Lanolin is a sensitive copy of your own skin oil and can be mixed into oils and lotions for extra nourishment.

Essential Oils for Ageing Skin Care

Add a few drops – between 3 and 9 according to how strong you want it – of one or two of the following essential oils to 15ml of your chosen base oil for further effect. All of these improve the condition of tired or ageing skin: **frankincense, geranium, lavender, neroli, patchouli, rose, sandalwood.**

Facial for Tired Skin

This leaves the face feeling fantastically soft.

2 tbs ripe avocado, mashed

1 tsp each clear honey, lemon juice and yoghurt

Mix together. Wrap a towel around your shoulders and apply to the face. Lie down for 10 minutes, and relax. Allow it all to soak in, then wipe off with a damp soft cloth. Finish with a toner such as rose water.

You can also use tahini (sesame paste) as a face mask: mix it to a useable consistency with a few drops of cider vinegar, and apply as above. Its protein nourishes and its oiliness lubricates, adding vitality to the skin.

Anti-wrinkle Cream

You can buy beeswax and lanolin from mail-order firms (see Resources, page 202) in the business of aromatherapy products, as well as some specialist pharmacists. This aromatic cream enriches the skin and keeps it deliciously smooth.

12g (¹/₂oz) beeswax

50g (2fl oz) lanolin

100g (4fl oz) coconut oil

50g (2oz) almond oil

30ml (1fl oz) orange flower water

3 drops tincture of benzoin or frankincense essential oil

Melt the beeswax with the lanolin in a bowl over hot water. Add in the oils and stir well. Gradually add the flower water, stirring so that it amalgamates. Off the heat, add the essential oil and beat briskly until smooth and creamy. Pot and seal.

Using the fingertips, dab tiny amounts on to the orbital bone and around the eyes.

Top Tips

- Keep an atomiser spray of water by your mirror and lightly mist the face before applying creams, which will then keep the moisture in.
- Add a few drops of cider vinegar to all your skin treatments: it tones the skin, helps flakiness and excess dryness.
- Soured cream is excellent for dry skin: use it as a face splash or add to your facial (see above).
- If you drink nettle tea and/or comfrey tea, your skin will not wrinkle, according to country wisdom. A face pack of pulped apples works wonders too, apparently!

Eyes

The skin around the eyes is tissue-paper thin, thinner than on any other part of the body. Because of this delicacy it shows wear and tear earlier than other skin, developing fine lines and wrinkles from the 20s onwards. There are ways of protecting this fragile area.

- Wear dark glasses to shield the eyes.
- Apply small amounts of sun-protection factor cream, or use a moisturiser that contains it.
- Never use soap on this area: use a gentle cleanser.
- Don't smoke
- Take regular exercise.
- Get the amount of sleep that you need.
- Don't use creams which contain fragrances on the eye zone, because they often trigger sensitivity. The same is also true of some emulsifiers and emollients.
- Use a specially designed eye-zone product at night.
- Don't use heavy, oily creams, or put any cream on too thickly in this area because it cannot absorb well and the skin pores get blocked.
- Avoid using paper tissues around the eye area because they can scratch the delicate skin. Use soft cotton pads instead, preferably organic

ones since the non-organic ones are heavy in pesticides and bleach and can trigger reactions.

- Don't rub the skin or drag it about with the fingertips when applying creams (or at any other time). Just dot your eye-zone cream along the orbital bone and tap it in: the fine lines will act as conduits to absorb the moisture without your help.

Home Treatments

- Drop two camomile teabags into boiling water, add a few drops of cider vinegar, then remove and cool. Lie down on the bed or sofa for at least 10 minutes with the cold teabags on your eyes. Deeply refreshing, and guaranteed to reduce puffiness and dark circles under the eyes.
- Peel a short piece of cucumber and slice it thinly. Lie down and place one slice over each eye and lie there for several minutes. Then replace with another two slices to get the coolness again. Cucumber is not only refreshing for the eyes but also reduces eye strain.
- For tired eyes, lightly moisten two cotton pads with witch-hazel, and lie down with them over the eyes. Rest for 5-10 minutes.

The Eye Bag

One of life's most simple but delicious treats is resting with a silk eye bag over your eyes.

Cut two scraps of silk into rectangles about 19 x 6cm (7^1/2 x 2^1/2in). Sew it up along both long sides and one short side,

Cold teabags are deeply refreshing for the eyes.

Cucumber cools and relieves tired eyes.

leaving a seam allowance of ¹/2cm (¹/4in). Turn inside out neatly. Fill with 125g (4¹/2oz) rice, with a few fresh lavender buds added. Sew up the fourth side.

Place this fragrant bag over the eyes when lying on your back in bed or on the sofa, or in any of the supine positions for yoga (pages 128 and 162).

Teeth

Healthy teeth are an important item on the agenda, the more so as you grow older. Good dental care is simple, it's only a matter of awareness and routine. Bad teeth and gums are not only painful, and sometimes lead to complications, but also increase the risk of developing halitosis (see below). Halitosis can lose you friends, jobs and lovers, so the social importance of dental hygiene is paramount!

Top Tips for Teeth

- Avoid eating too many sugary foods or drinking sugary drinks.
- Brush your teeth every morning and evening to remove the layer of bacteria and debris or plaque that builds up, which otherwise hardens into tartar which has to be scraped off by a dentist.
- Don't over-brush: 'scrubbing' your teeth, particularly the front teeth, destroys the enamel.
- Use a small-headed toothbrush and replace it once a month.
- Slooshing your mouth out with water or an alcohol-free mouthwash before brushing minimises the need to 'scrub' since it does much to wash away the bacteria.

- If you live in an area that does not have added fluoride in the water, use a fluoride mouthwash regularly to protect the enamel. This also improves the breath.
- Eat calcium-rich foods – skimmed milk is an excellent source.
- Floss regularly every evening. This is important, since much food matter gets into crevices where the brush cannot reach, and if not removed can rot and lead to infection (let alone bad breath).
- Have regular check-ups with your dentist.
- If your teeth are discoloured or uneven or causing problems, consult your dentist about the possibilities of orthodontics, veneers, crowns or bonding, amalgams etc.

Halitosis

There are certain people – and they tend to be in the older age group – who we cringe from getting too close to because of their bad breath. Halitosis is caused by excess bacteria in the mouth, and can increase if you don't take exercise.

Is it you?

- Lick the underside of your wrist with the back of the tongue (as far back as you can reach), wait a couple of seconds and then sniff.
- Rub a tissue on the back part of the tongue and do the sniff test.
- Do the sniff test on your floss after using it.

What to do about halitosis

- Brush and floss regularly..
- Drink masses of water daily
- Take aerobic exercise (page 132).
- Use an alcohol-free mouthwash.
- Buy a tongue-cleaner from the pharmacist and scrape the tongue daily.
- Chew sugarless gum.
- Or chew cinnamon, cloves or parsley which all do the trick.

Looking after your hair

More than any one other feature, your hair defines your 'look'. There is power in hair and has been ever since Delilah cut Samson's locks. An important key to healthy hair is good nutrition, as is keeping stress at tolerable levels. Above all, though, befriending a good hairdresser and allowing her/him to be your ally is probably the best move you can make. Once you have found one that you like and trust, treat yourself to regular sessions so that your hair is well cut and looked after.

In between times, here are some tips for bringing gloss and bounce and life into your hair.

- Gently heat a little extra-virgin olive oil and massage into dry hair. Wrap in a towel and leave to soak in for at least 30 minutes before shampooing.
- Use bristle brushes and good quality combs, avoiding nylon which puts static into hair.
- Brush your hair thoroughly every day: brushing releases the natural oils and keeps it glossy.
- Give yourself a scalp massage from time to time, using borage oil or sunflower oil. Take the fingers in strong circular movements for 2-3 minutes, then shampoo out afterwards.
- Don't over-use the hair drier, otherwise your hair can be damaged by the heat, becoming brittle and breaking easily. Allow to dry naturally if possible.
- Avoid using harsh chemicals in your hair. Use natural vegetable products (read the label – if there is one!) and buy organic products to avoid chemical overload.
- If your hair is dull and thin, try taking zinc supplements since your level may be low.
- Don't over-expose the hair to sunshine (wear a hat or scarf) or central heating, which dries it out.
- Don't wring your hair out hard after washing, because it is weak when wet and prone to break. Just squeeze gently before wrapping your head in a towel.
- For frizzy hair, rub a little baby oil or almond oil into your hands and smooth them over the hair. Brush in gently.
- Don't overdo the shampoo on the scalp: use less than recommended on the bottle because the too much of the detergent in it can damage your hair
- Likewise, don't overdo the conditioner on the tips: too much leaves your hair flat and lifeless.
- Always rinse very thoroughly indeed. Add lemon to the final rinse, in a basin, to restore the hair's acid mantle.
- Blow-dry the hair in the opposite way to its direction of growth, to give it body.

Feed the Follicles

Two excellent home-made conditioners to nourish your scalp and make your hair glossy.

Banana conditioner

Mash 1 ripe banana with a tablespoon of sunflower oil and ½ teaspoon lemon juice. Massage into dry hair. Leave on for 20 to 30 minutes before shampooing out. The potassium in the banana nourishes the scalp, the oil conditions dry hair and skin, and the lemon restores the acid-alkali balance.

Revitalising oil

30ml (1fl oz) extra-virgin olive oil

2 tsp jojoba oil

2 tsp wheatgerm oil

8 drops geranium essential oil

12 drops lavender essential oil

6 drops patchouli essential oil

Pour the vegetable oils into a clean 50ml (2fl oz) bottle, add the essential oils and shake well. Apply small amounts of the oil to dampened hair, massage in well, and wrap in a towel for at least 30 minutes before shampooing out. Repeat the treatment once a month. This deliciously aromatic conditioner brings shine and body to dull or damaged hair.

Greying Hair

The big question: to leave the grey in, or not to leave the grey in? The final decision is of course personal, but it is worth *not* rushing into a change of colour impulsively at that moment when you catch yourself unawares in a mirror and are aghast at the ageing you. Look at the options and discuss them with your ally the hairdresser first. Be careful about home-dyes: they often do not come out quite as you would expect from looking at the model on the packaging... Here are some of the options.

- Get your hairdresser to put in a few highlights or lowlights.
- Use a vegetable rinse (not a chemical dye) to mask the grey areas.
- Have a semi-permanent colour put on that lasts for about 24 washes.
- Get your hairdresser to put on a permanent dye which entails re-doing the roots from time to time. (Bear in mind that there have been cancer-scares about hair dyes. The advantage of highlights and lowlights is that they are not applied to the scalp, but only to the hair.)
- Stay 'au naturel'. You may be one of the lucky ones whose grey or white is evenly distributed, or total, and looks beautiful.

Thinning Hair

Hair usually starts to grow less thickly well before your 50s: thinning is a natural event. However, excessive thinning can be caused by stress, by a bad diet or by missing meals regularly, or by poor circulation which can be improved with exercise. All of these are things you can do something about. You can also help it cosmetically: to give your hair the impression of body and thickness, use volumisers which you apply to wet hair before blow-drying. They are non-sticky and leave a protective film around the hairs, giving them bounce and shine.

Hands and nails

Our hands are one of the busiest places in the body. They work hard for us and are on constant active duty. No wonder then that they show their age – the more so if we neglect them. The skin is thinner than on other parts of the body and requires special care, particularly since it may be subjected to immersion in water several times a day. This has the effect of paint-stripper, stripping what oils there are away and leaving the hands dried out. Water weakens nails too in exactly the same way. It has been said that the hands are the windows to the soul: perhaps our hands say more about us than we realise, and are due for more attention than we bother with normally.

Look After Your Hands

- Wear lined rubber gloves whenever you need to put your hands in water (direct contact with rubber softens nails).
- Use handcreams that do not contain alcohol

(this dries out the skin). Creams containing an SPF are best (age-spots fade if hands are not exposed to UV light).

- Keep pots of handcream everywhere in the house, especially near basins, and also in your bag so that you can apply it throughout the day.
- Have regular manicures, or give yourself home-manicures.
- Protect your hands with gloves while gardening.
- If hands become especially dry, rub several drops of jojoba or almond oil into them and massage well.
- Give your hands impromptu massage from time to time, pulling the fingers, pushing them backwards, and digging one thumb into the opposite palm.
- Do the dog pose (see page 162) really stretching the fingers and pressing the palms of the hand to the floor.

Look After Your Nails

- If your nails are weak, apply almond oil once a week: just moisten a cotton bud with the oil, dab it on, let it soak in for a little before massaging it in, pushing back the cuticles at the same time.
- Wear lined rubber gloves when immersing hands in water (see above).
- Polish your nails once a week, using a buffer.
- Take evening primrose for healthy nails.
- Rub cocoa butter into cuticles before pushing them back gently with an orange stick.
- If you have white spots on your nails, you may

need to take a zinc supplement.

- Nails in very bad condition can be improved by taking the vitamin biotin over a period of 6 months as the new growth comes through.
- Use an acetone-free nail polish remover: acetone leaves your nails prone to splitting.
- If your nails are weak, use a strengthening base coat before applying polish. Polish is good to help strengthen nails, but leave it off for a few days a month to allow air to get to the nails.
- Eat parsnips and parsley for healthy nails, according to country wisdom!

Feet

The skin on the feet produces no natural oils at all so it has the most need of moisturising. Yet most of us behave as if we haven't *got* feet: they are locked up in prisons of shoes all their lives and horribly neglected. It's only when something goes wrong with them that we realise how precious they are. The skin becomes dry and cracked, and the nails brittle and unsightly. We may walk up to 113,000km (roughly 70,000 miles) in a lifetime, so the poor feet deserve a bit of tlc. Uncared-for feet become ugly, but cherished feet look lovely. They require more care and not less as we age.

Looking After Your Feet

- Moisturise them regularly, once a day if possible, preferably after showering or bathing.
- Massage your feet regularly: pull the toes,

stretch them back, and press deep into the soles of the feet with your thumb, following the lines of the bones from heel to toe pads.

- Remove hard or rough skin with pumice, which is more natural and less abrasive than a foot file.
- Wear comfortable shoes: if your feet are killing you your whole body is affected.
- Check that your shoe size hasn't changed: often feet become broader as we get older (gravity!)
- Wear socked feet or walk barefoot around the house, to give your feet the chance to relax and be natural. Clogs are better than closed shoes.
- Go for regular sessions with a chiropodist
- Treat yourself to regular pedicures.
- Apply almond oil to the nails (see above).
- Indulge in the occasional reflexology treatment: it relaxes the feet beautifully.
- Give yourself foot baths: soak your feet in warm water to which you can add almond or jojoba oil, and essential oils such as benzoin, lavender, geranium, lemon, peppermint or any other favourite, about 10 drops in all. After 10 minutes or so, wrap them in a towel, then dry off and apply some moisturising cream. You can buy mini foot-spas with a whirlpool action and knobbly floor which massages and releases the feet like nothing else. They are not that expensive and are a great luxury. Spoil yourself!

Pamper yourself

Your bathroom is an opportunity for self-indulgence. Don't miss it! Decorate it in your favourite colour – I did mine out in restful shades of sea blues and deep lavender, installed candles, and stocked the shelves with fragrant oils. It transformed my life. The towels now hang in front of the radiator so that they are always deliciously warm. This is where hydrotherapy takes place on a regular basis, and how reviving it is. Water is a wonderful cosmetic as well as a great restorer and relaxant, and you can add touches of luxury with softening oils and fragrant flower aromas. (I avoid 'foam baths' because they contain detergent: great for cleaning the bath, I'm not so sure about my skin.)

Best Baths

- Take a bath at any time of the day that pleases you: secret pleasures are the best.
- Add cider vinegar (a small cupful) to your bath regularly. It restores energy and softens the skin. It is also a useful treatment for thrush.
- Add a tablespoon or two of almond oil to the water to soften the skin.
- Add 5-10 drops of your chosen essential oils to the bath once it has finished running, so that they float on the surface and can release their aromas fully. You can combine up to 3 at a time, but don't exceed 12 drops in total. Essential oils are powerful.
- Light candles and turn off any electric light.
- If you like to read in the bath, which I do, this is how: keep your hands dry as you get into the water, hold the book above danger level, and then the only other thing is not to drop it into the bath... Leave the washing to the end. This is called Bliss.
- When you have finished, wrap yourself in a radiator-warmed towel to dry.

Oils to Relax With

Lavender is one of the best and most popular oils, for good reason. Ever since the time of the Romans it has been recognised for its quietening effects on an over-active brain, and as a sedative before sleeping. In country wisdom, rosemary is said to make the old young again. Worth a try. It is an excellent muscle relaxant and helps with aches and pains generally. Other oils to relax with are: basil, bergamot, camomile, cedarwood, frankincense, hyssop, juniper, marjoram, melissa, neroli, patchouli, sage, sandalwood, ylang-ylang.

Oils good for lifting the mood are sandalwood, jasmine (a great favourite but very expensive!), rose (cosmically costly) and bergamot.

One of the best investments you can make in your well-being is to spoil yourself to a session (a weekend...a week...) at a health spa. There you can relax and luxuriate in a wide variety of treatments (from sauna, steamroom and jacuzzi to hydrotherapy baths with seaweed treatments, thalassotherapy, mud treatments, paraffin wax treatments, lymphatic drainage massages and Thai or Swedish massages) that replenish your energy and vitality, leaving you with a wonderful feel-good factor as you return to the 'real' world.

vital
health
checks

vital health checks

If we are to be well, we must look after ourselves Germaine Greer

A 1999 MORI survey conducted in the UK found that 63 per cent of over-50s never exercise, 74 per cent never participate in sport and that over half of them are overweight or obese. Arthritis, high blood pressure, insomnia, angina and digestive disorders assail them. Tea, biscuits and soup are staples of their diet although most of them know that pasta and fresh vegetables are better for them. What kind of role model is a badly-nourished couch potato?

Scientific evidence points to the importance of good nutrition and moderate exercise in maintaining health and minimising the risk of serious disease. Playing card games and going shopping, eating fried meals and processed snacks, are not habits that are likely to improve our chances. You have to work intelligently at being healthy and keeping in shape. There are benefits to be reaped from a change in lifestyle at almost any age, and it is up to you to take responsibility for this part of the journey.

The quality of your life is dependent not on others but on you. Nobody else can do your eating for you; nobody else can take your exercise for you. You need to keep your body in good working order to maintain health because it is more precious than wealth. Some do: a record number (1300) of over-50s entered the first London marathon of the 21st century, an increase of more than 30 per cent since 1995. Awesome.

Not all illnesses or disabilities are an *unavoidable* part of ageing. The all-too-common infirmities of osteoporosis, muscle weakness, loss of balance, heart disease, increased blood pressure and diabetes are not inevitable. We may passively assume that they are, and allow ourselves to become the victims of ageing, but if we are honest, and look at our 'health habits' truthfully, we may be able to see what we can do about improving them and becoming the masters of our destiny. If you are overweight, smoke, drink too much, or take very little exercise, you are stacking heavy burdens on to

your poor body. You are as old – or as young – as your body feels. And there is a lot you can do about that. The resources you need to keep physically and mentally fit are instantly available.

It is never too late to start. Our skin replaces itself every month, the stomach lining every five days, the liver every six weeks, the skeleton every three months. In the course of one year, 98 per cent of the atoms in your body will be exchanged for new ones. Think of the power you have to dictate the quality of those atoms by watching how you treat your body! New and healthy habits have been shown to be a remarkable antidote to hard living. We have choices. And time. You can always make time for things that are important.

Most centenarians don't smoke and have never been obese, and have remained physically and mentally active. By staying healthy and vital, you can also have a positive effect on those around you: your vitality will do much to change any ageist attitudes lurking in their minds. You will, one person at a time, decrease the load on the medical health services. Both are a valuable contribution to society.

To do this you need information and support. There is no shortage of health education for all age groups in newspapers and periodicals, libraries and on the Internet. If support is not to be had through family and social networks, you can seek it through health professionals. An understanding family doctor, homeopath, aromatherapist, herbalist, yoga teacher, masseuse and many others can help us to find a healthy lifestyle

Life should be fun, emotionally satisfying as well as physically healthy, because the spirit as well as the body needs the right nourishment. A sense of well-being, of being relaxed about life, a spiritual practice, having a good time with family and friends, and believing in the axiom 'a little of what you fancy does you good' goes a long way to maintaining good health. A balance of all these elements leads to serenity and contentment. The right food, balance in exercise, work and leisure, the right amount of sleep and rest, the enjoyment of pleasure without excess in drinking and socialising, can bring harmony into our lives. Everything starts and ends with the body: if your body is out of sorts, your mind and spirit struggle. Look after it. It's the only one you've got.

How should I start?

Think of your body as a long-term investment. Start now: it is never too late.

- Take up a form of exercise that you enjoy (see pages 119–32). Increased disability in later life is frequently due to muscular weakness.
- Coronary heart disease kills one fifth of women over 50. If you eat a diet high in saturated fats and salt, change your diet (see pages 137–47). If you have a family history of heart disease, consult your doctor about how to minimise the chances of contracting it.
- Give up smoking today: smoking causes cancer. It can also give you emphysema and other respiratory diseases. It makes you breathless

and impairs fitness. It depresses your appetite and inhibits vitamin absorption. It dries out and wrinkles facial skin, smells horrible, and is expensive. It pollutes the atmosphere around you to the extent that other people can suffer from smoking-related conditions even though they don't smoke.

- Drink lots of water (see page 139).
- Attend regular hearing checks, eyesight tests and dental care.
- Look after your oral health: flossing your teeth and caring for your gums reduces the risk of infections that can affect the heart (see page 105).
- Schedule regular screenings: cervical smears, mammograms and bone density scans.
- Have your GP check your blood pressure and cholesterol levels annually.
- Check your weight. If you need to lose some, check your diet and plan a better way of eating.
- Eating regular servings daily of fresh fruit and vegetables reduces the risk of developing most chronic diseases.
- If you are not sleeping well, reduce your intake of coffee and/or alcohol, look at your eating habits (see page 137-8), and establish a restful routine around bedtime (see page 134).

How to live happily to 100

- Visualise how you want to be at 100 and keep it in view.
- Learn to relax and have fun.
- Maintain a busy social life.
- Cut down your coffee intake to one cup a day.
- Don't over-expose your skin to the sun.
- Drink a couple of glasses of wine a day, and lots of water.
- Floss your teeth and keep your body clean.
- Avoid accidents: use your seat belt and watch your step.
- Eat frugally but follow a healthy diet.
- Get out into the fresh air – lots.
- Don't believe the hype about youth-enhancing products.
- Keep fit, but also get enough rest.
- Read a lot, keep learning and try to keep mentally active.
- Follow your chosen spiritual path.

The right exercise

Champions take responsibility. When the ball comes over the net, you can be sure I want the ball Billie Jean King

My friend Elsa was invited to go on a hike while she and her husband were guests at a corporate convention in the USA. While the menfolk were engaged in business, the women convened at the hostess's beautiful suburban home, attired in shellsuits and trainers. The sun was shining and the air fresh. Two large dogs were straining on their leashes, ready for the off. The women

Warm-up, cool-down exercises

It is vitally important to stretch before exercising - to warm up the muscles – and afterwards to stretch them out and to loosen joints which may be affected by the impact of the exercise. This series of stretches works on all the important muscle groups involved in average-level exercise.

1. Calf muscles
Feet hip-width apart, elbows to wall, tailbone tucked under, breathe

2. Quadriceps
Stand on one leg, pull other heel back to buttock, keep knees together, breathe

3. Lateral stretch
Legs wide apart, feet straight, stretch body sideways, one hand to leg, other arm reaches over head, breathe

4. Groins and thighs
Legs wide, turn one foot outwards and bend the knee, drop into the hips, breathe

4b. then turn back foot and face bent knee, hands on knee, drop into hips, breathe

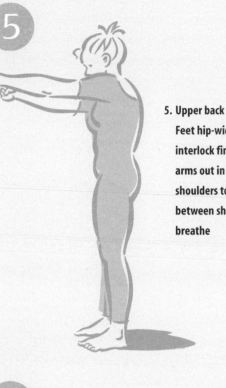

5

5. Upper back
Feet hip-width apart,
interlock fingers, stretch
arms out in front, round
shoulders to open up
between shoulder blades,
breathe

6

6. Shoulders
Feet together, one arm
up the back between
shoulder blades, other
hand over shoulder to
hold hands behind back
(if you can't reach, place
upper hand flat on back
of neck, or lower)

7

7. Hamstrings
Lie flat on back, take one leg towards you,
knee slightly bent, pull foot towards head,
breathe

8

8. Lower back
Lie on back, hug knees to chest, stretch
arms out on floor at shoulder level,
take knees to one side towards arm,
relax legs down, turn head to look
along other arm, breathe

gathered at the front door and set off down the circular gravel drive that swept around a manicured lawn. Walking briskly, they passed the gate and went full circle, whereupon the hostess, a woman of ample girth, bent down to place a pebble on the manorial front step. 'They're for counting our rounds,' she explained as they set off briskly again, chattering breathlessly, on their second circuit. And so it went, this hike of overfed ladies, around and around, until a small pile of pebbles had accumulated and they retired indoors for coffee and apparently much-needed muffins.

Better than nothing, perhaps, but not that impressive. Research into exercise shows that 12 weeks' regular exercise at a fairly intense level (see opposite) radically increases fitness in older people, with psychological benefits too. Whereas exercising in your 20s and 30s makes little difference to overall health, doing so in your 40s makes a big difference and in your 50s upwards a huge difference. In 2000 the Oxford Dementia Centre reported the case of a patient with severe dementia whose programme of fitness training, swimming and rock climbing enabled him to start speaking fluent Italian again, a language he had forgotten for years, and of another who began composing classical music. Experiments on 80-year-olds who had never exercised, making them go through a rigorous and regular regime, showed that it made a huge difference to their health, sense of well-being, and cognitive function.

Your body is a machine: treat it like one. If you don't look after your car it doesn't run properly and it deteriorates. The same applies to the body. Use it or lose it, keep it serviced, keep it running! One year of activity can claim back ten years of inactivity. Active ageing makes all the difference, yet 40 per cent of the over-50s are inactive. On which side of the line do you fall?

Why Exercise?

- The functional capacity both physical and mental of a well-exercised person over 50 is phenomenally superior to that of a similar non-exercised person.
- Exercise increases your life expectancy: the fittest people live the longest.
- Regular aerobic exercise lifts the spirits and makes you feel more cheerful. Depression is a serious complaint among older women, dramatically increasing the risk of a stroke so this is another important aspect of exercise.
- Exercise builds up bone density. This means that you are less likely to fracture bones in an accident, and to suffer back pain.
- Aerobic exercise improves your stamina, helps you recover more quickly when you rest, and keeps your heart and lungs younger for longer.
- Exercise pays big dividends: heart, lungs, muscles, posture, bones, trimness, appetite and sleep all benefit.
- You are less likely to fall if your muscles are well toned: most falls in older people are due to muscular weakness.
- Keeping your muscles strong means that you

can do simple things like getting out of chairs with grace rather than difficulty. The more you use them, the stronger they get.

- The effects of exercise mean that you will maintain your independence longer: you'll remain able-bodied and mobile.
- Exercise staves off the ravages of mental decay in old age. It improves oxygen flow to the brain, increasing your alertness, memory and problem-solving abilities.
- Exercise increases metabolism and burns off body fat.
- Tests have shown that if you are really fit you measure 15 years younger than your biological age. Keeping fit keeps you looking younger.
- The effects of exercise improve balance and stabilise blood sugar levels.
- Exercise reduces the risk of coronary heart disease, one of the principal killers of women over 50.
- Exercise keeps you toned and flexible. You'll have more stamina, strength, suppleness and co-ordination.
- It improves self-esteem because you both look and feel better.

How Much Do I Need to Exercise?

You should try to exercise for about 20-30 minutes at least 3 times a week. It's not much. Take a brisk early morning walk, or play tennis before lunch, or do a yoga practice in the afternoon, or go cycling or swimming before

The right amount of exercise helps you keep healthy as you age.

dinner. Establish a routine for yourself that suits your daily programme, but don't go and ruin it all at the weekend: if you turn into a couch potato all Saturday and Sunday, the effects are quickly lost.

Having said that, too much exercise can also be deleterious, leading to oxygen toxicity and the release of free radicals and lactic acid into the bloodstream. It can stress your joints, may strain or tear muscles, and through sweating too much you may lose minerals and other essential nutrients. Older athletes are found to suffer to a greater degree from osteoarthritis than those who take gentler forms of exercise.

Which Form of Exercise is Best?

The best form of exercise is that which suits your fitness level and temperament the best, and the one that you enjoy the most. Taking exercise that your body is not prepared for, or which stresses you mentally (or bores you) is a non-starter. Find something that you really look forward to doing.

Some General Guidelines

- Start gently. Don't overdo it, but build up gradually.
- Train yourself to be more active in everyday life: use the stairs rather than the lift, walk to the shops, cycle instead of driving short distances, and rather than waiting for the bus walk to the next stop.
- If you are uncertain, or have particular health problems, check with your doctor first.
- Make sure that you go to a well-qualified instructor. Word of mouth is often the best recommendation. Bad or inexperienced instruction can damage your body.
- If something hurts, stop. Forget 'no pain no gain' over the age of 45.
- Keep your commitment to exercise regularly. The benefits are not maintained if you stop-start. Most people find it helpful to exercise in a group, because it helps to maintain enthusiasm, and has the added value of being sociable and enjoyable.
- Include some cardiovascular work: gentle aerobic exercise – even brisk walking or climbing stairs are immensely beneficial.
- Tools of the trade: make sure you get the right equipment, the right shoes or trainers for dancing or walking, a non-slip mat for yoga etc.
- An instruction video at home to practise between classes can be useful, although not ideal since there is nobody to check that you are doing it correctly.
- Do warm-up stretches both before and after exercise (see page 120).
- Drink lots of water to replace lost fluids: running uses up 600ml (24fl oz) per hour.

How to Find Your Local Classes

Word of mouth is the best recommendation. Or contact your:

- local leisure centre or other local facilities

- library
- gym
- local sports shop
- tourist office
- local newspaper
  (See also Resources, page 202)

Yoga

Yoga has withstood the test of time. Anything that is still going after 5000 years has to have something in it. It originated in the Himalayas where, as legend goes, the gods passed it down to the holy men of the mountains. The practice is rooted in stilling the mind, and the word yoga means union: integrating mind, soul and body in order to unite with the divine. The postures that developed out of this ethical philosophy keep the body flexible and co-ordinated, strong and mobile, the muscles toned, the mind balanced, calm and alert, and the spirit awakened. Yoga also alleviates and prevents arthritis and other conditions associated with ageing. It keeps stress levels down and help you sleep better. Find a good teacher who suits your level and understanding, and establish a daily practice for yourself, of anything from 10 minutes to an hour. (See Resources, page 202.)

Pilates

This method, developed in the 1920s by Joseph Pilates – sportsman and physical trainer – tones and aligns the body by working on deep postural muscles. It can help rehabilitation after injury, and helps to remedy back pain. It also improves fitness, flexibility, strength, joint mobility, co-ordination, posture, balance and alignment. The movements are controlled from the abdominal centre, with the pelvic floor muscles engaged. They are carried out in a flowing, relaxed and focused way in co-ordination with the breathing.

Do make sure that your Pilates teacher has a valid qualification from an authentic trainer, and has done more than a couple of weekends' training. The work is strong, and inadequate instruction can do more harm than good. (See Resources page 204.)

Maka Ho: a Daily Stretch

The exercises (pages 126-7) work on all the different meridian lines or energy channels of the body. They are based on the Japanese practice of shiatsu and their effect is amazing in terms of energising, balancing you and increasing suppleness. Just take between 5 and 10 minutes each morning (some of the positions may feel really difficult to start with, but within a week or two you will feel the difference in your body's ability to stretch, even first thing in the morning). They feel easier after bathing or showering since the body relaxes and is loosened up by the warm water. Even if you take no other form of exercise, these stretches will bring remarkable benefits.

Take two deep breaths in each stretch. More if you have time.

Maka Ho

Doing this sequence takes just a few minutes each morning and has an astounding effect on suppleness as well as energy supply! Remember to take at least two deep breaths in each position.

1. Feet hip-width apart, interlock fingers behind back, fold trunk over legs bringing arms back behind you

2. Kneel, then take feet apart keeping knees together and sit between heels, interlock fingers, stretch arms up and drop head back. Then go back on to elbows and finally on to top of head, clasping elbows behind

3. Sit upright with soles of feet together close in towards hips, hold feet . Then stretch forward and bring head towards feet

4. Stretch both legs out in front, fold at the hips and stretch forwards, relax head down, hands resting beside legs on floor

5. Sit cross-legged (or in lotus position), cross your arms, breathe, bend forward, drop head into forearms. Repeat, changing the cross of the arms and the legs

6. Sit with legs wide, stretch trunk over each leg in turn, holding leg or foot, relax the head

7. Sit with legs wide, twist body and stretch sideways over extended leg, bringing top arm over the head

Relax and destress

A series of yoga asanas that restores and invigorates as it balances the body and mind, these are gentle stretches into which you can breathe and relax.

1

1. Legs up the wall
Sit with one hip touching the wall, take legs up wall as you swing body round to floor at right angles to wall, make sure you are straight, stretch arms behind head, close eyes, breathe

2. Triangle
Take legs about 1m (3ft) apart, turn one foot out, stretch sideways, take lower hand down to leg and other arm up to the vertical, breathe

2

3. Warrior
Take feet very wide, turn one foot out and bend knee keeping it in line with the foot, sink into hips, keep trunk vertical, arms stretching horizontally, breathe

3

4

4. Head to knee with shoulder stretch
Feet hip-width apart and straight, hands into prayer position behind back, take one foot forward, take weight on to back heel, stretch over front leg, relax head, elbows up, breathe

5. Camel
Kneel up with knees hip
width apart, keep hips
forward as you lean back
off tailbone, bring hands
to feet, relax head back,
eyes soft, breathe

6. Bridge
Lie on back, heels close to hips, arms beside
body palms down, contract buttock muscles
to lift hips until weight is back on shoulders,
breathe

7. Lower back
Lie on back, hug knees to chest,
stretch arms out on floor at shoulder
level, take knees to one side towards
arm, relax legs down, turn head to
look along other arm, breathe

8. Child
Sit back on heels kneeling, bend
forwards at hips, bring head
down to floor, relax shoulders,
drop arms, relax face, breathe

Salute to the sun

This ancient salutation contains big stretches and amounts to quite vigorous exercise. Following the drawings, practise connecting the postures with the breath and work so that they flow into one another like a dance. The effect is revitalising, converting negative energy into positive energy.

1

2

2. Breathe in, back arch

1. Hands in prayer position, breathe in, breathe out

3

3. Breathe out, forward bend

4. Breathe in – take right foot forward into the lunge

5. Dog pose (p. 163) Breathe out,

4

5

6. Snake
Breathe in

7. Cobra
Breathe out, breathe
in

9. Breathe in – take
right foot forward
into the lunge

8. Dog pose (p. 163)
Breathe out,

10. Breathe out,
forward bend

11. Breathe in,
back arch

12. Breathe out, in,
take a few
breaths before
repeating,
taking the left
leg forward in
the lunges 4
and 9

Tai Chi

Tai Chi is an ancient Chinese system of stretches and balances that improves co-ordination, balance and strength. It relaxes and focuses the mind, frees the joints, extends the muscles and calms both mind and body. A study in Atlanta, Georgia found that older people taking part in a 15-week Tai Chi programme reduced their risk of falling by nearly 50 per cent.

Walking

Walking is one of the best forms of exercise, and is safe for all levels of fitness. As well as working the body and breath (taken at a good pace), it settles the mind and brings a sense of serenity and perspective. If you can get out into the countryside, or a beautiful park, the benefits are even better, with the added value of connecting with nature and breathing fresh air.

Start with a brisk 10 minutes, walking to a pace where you feel slightly breathless but still able to hold a conversation. Gradually build up the distance and speed, and even include little bursts of jogging. Wear quality trainers with good impact-absorption and ankle support.

Other Options

You may prefer more active types of sport, in which case the following are all suitable to take up in this stage of your life – so long as you get a good instructor, and take it easy to start with. It is important to do the stretches (see page 120) both before and after strenuous exercise, to warm up the muscles, and to cool down afterwards:

- swimming
- running
- cycling
- dancing
- rebounding (a simple form of trampolining)
- tennis
- badminton
- martial arts
- skiing
- watersports
- keep-fit classes
- archery
- croquet

Note: if you suffer or have suffered from a heart condition, severe back pain, high blood pressure or are recovering from an operation, take your doctor's advice before embarking on any form of exercise.

Sleep and relaxation

*Come, Sleep! O Sleep, the
certain knot of peace
The baiting place of wit, the
balm of woe,
The poor man's wealth, the
prisoner's release ...*
Sir Philip Sidney

There are four stages of sleep as brainwave activity slows down into deep sleep. These are punctuated by short periods of REM (rapid eye movement). As we get older our rapid-eye-movement sleep becomes lighter: we are more sensitive to disturbance, and more easily awakened. As time goes on we get less and less of the deeply restful fourth stage of sleep, the slow-wave oblivion that is so refreshing and which came so easily in youth. This stage of sleep transforms mood and energies, it wipes the mental and physical slate clean, and has been shown to increase after exercise and by fasting.

If we fail to adapt to the different patterns that come with age, we set up deleterious habits that put a strain on our minds and bodies. It is important to ride with the changes in our daily needs and rhythms. We don't always need as much sleep as we think: Margaret Thatcher managed with only four to five hours a night when she was prime minister.

Look on less sleep as a positive thing: it frees up so much more time! Sleeping too much can slow you down and make you feel groggy, dulling your responses and clouding your mind. Poor sleeping patterns do not constitute illness. However, chronic lack of sleep does speed up the process of ageing and makes you feel (and look!) terrible. It causes irritability, daytime sleepiness, headaches, mental confusion, impaired memory, and as well as making you function poorly at work it puts a strain on relationships. However, the following are steps that you can take to help yourself.

Thinking It Through

- Accept that you don't need as much sleep as you used to: the necessity for sleep diminishes with age. Decide what to do with the extra time and establish new routines accordingly.
- Sometimes insomnia is rooted in depression, sometimes in unwanted weight loss. If you suspect either to be the case, seek help.
- Work out how many hours sleep you think you need in order to function best: too much will make you dozy and lethargic, too little will leave you exhausted and irritable.
- Analyse your natural biorhythms, as to when your energy levels peak and when they are at their lowest, and work out the best waking/sleeping cycles for you. Go with the changing pattern of your life rhythms (see Resources, page 204).
- Accept that sleep is season-related. Most of us need less in the summer and more in the winter.
- Always get up at the same time in the morning, however badly you have slept, otherwise your body can never establish a regular pattern.
- How many years have you been using that mattress? Does it give you the support and/or the restfulness that you now require? Check your bedding too: perhaps the duvet is too warm or not warm enough, and the pillows too plump and not giving your neck enough support.
- Establish a regular bedtime routine: a bath, a hot drink, an evening stroll, meditation (see page 71).

What Not to Do

- Don't use sleeping tablets. They are not the answer: they give you only shallow sleep during the night and a hangover the next day. You can become seriously dependent on them. If you have to take a pill, take herbal preparations based on valerian instead.

- Don't go to bed until you are sleepy, even if it is past your usual bedtime. Instead, read a book or watch a film to engage your mind and take it off whatever worries may keep you awake.

- Don't eat a large meal late in the evening: leave at least two hours between dinner and going to bed to digest your food.

- Don't drink alcohol late in the evening: it may make you feel drowsy at the time, but it will disturb your natural sleep patterns and will usually wake you up in the wee small hours.

- Reduce your daily caffeine intake: its effects are sometimes longer-lasting than you might expect. Avoid caffeine from late afternoon onwards (or altogether): this includes tea, chocolate and cola as well as coffee (and even decaffeinated coffee may have some caffeine content) which will keep you awake.

- Don't watch violent or frightening TV late into the evening. The mind may get to work on it during the night and lead to restlessness.

- Don't let your mind run away with you in the wakeful hours and take you around in its interminable circles: learn some breathing, relaxation and meditation techniques (see pages 136 and 71).

What to Do About Broken Sleep Patterns

- Take regular exercise during the day. An evening walk can be beneficial, and so can a gentle yoga practice before you go to bed, or meditation (see page 71).

- Always wait until you are sleepy before going to bed.

- Have a warm bath before bedtime. Raising the body temperature has been shown to promote good sleep. Put some drops of lavender essential oil into the water once the bath has run, for its soothing and relaxing properties.

- Drink a cup of camomile or lime blossom tea before retiring, or a hot milky drink.

- If you are menopausal, take black cohosh and/or agnus castus which regulate oestrogen levels and help to reduce those night sweats (see page 157) that disturb your rest.

- If light from the street disturbs you, wear an eye-mask. If there's too much noise, use ear-plugs to shut it out.

- Learn techniques of breathing, or of using the time productively (see below).

- Read something relaxing or peacefully entertaining before dropping off.

- If you are wakeful for long hours in the night, don't see it as a problem (otherwise it becomes one). Relish the deep peacefulness of the depths of night, and learn techniques to enjoy them rather than spending the time worrying that you will feel exhausted the next day.

- Schedule a catnap (call it a power-snooze if

you prefer) into your day. This short sleep can be really deep, and enormously refreshing.

- Try one or more of the following:
  - reading a good book
  - doing a crossword
  - meditating, wrapped up warm in a rug
  - breathing exercises
  - opening the window
  - writing a letter, or a diary
  - listening to the radio (have a Walkman by the bed so as not to disturb your partner)
  - listening to relaxation tapes (ditto)
  - doing a jigsaw puzzle
  - lying on your back and relaxing your body one bit at a time, starting at the scalp until you reach the toes
  - relishing the feel of the bed, the softness and warmth of the covers, telling yourself how much you enjoy the luxury of its comfort
  - staying resolutely in the present moment and following your breathing to stop your mind from raking up the past or anguishing about the future

One hour's sleep before midnight is worth two after
Proverb

Breathing Exercises

Balanced breathing soothes the nervous system and promotes sound sleep. Calming and centring, these exercises are a valuable resource.

Lying flat in bed

Rest one hand loosely on your chest and the other on your navel. Breathing quietly, inhale deeply and feel the slight rise of the abdomen under your hand. Exhale, making a quiet 'ah' sound, allowing the lower jaw to drop and feeling the other hand drop slightly. Breathe like this for as long as it takes to relax completely and for the mind to become quiet.

Sitting

1 Sitting comfortably with your back straight and lightly supported, breathe in and out, following your breath up and down the trunk in an imaginary line parallel to the spine. Fill up on the in-breath, empty on the out-breath. Keep your attention focused on the breath to the exclusion of everything else, so that at every moment you know that you are breathing in, or that you are breathing out.

2 A beautifully soothing exercise is to imagine the in-breath moving from the ground behind you up your spine, coming over your head and moving down the front of the body as you exhale, disappearing back into the ground. Enjoy the pause between the exhalation and the next inhalation as a space of silence and stillness.

3 Counting the breaths: count '1' on the first in and out breath, '2' on the second, and so on up to 10. If your attention wanders, and you only get up to 3 or 4 or whatever, return back to 1 again and see if you can get to 10. If you can, start at 1 again.

The right food

The beginning and end of all good is the pleasure of the stomach: even wisdom and culture must be referred to this
Epicurus

These days there's a risk that we have heard the litany of 'low-fat, low-sugar, high-fibre' so often that we don't heed it any more, let alone do anything about changing the more dubious of our habits. But now is the time, having arrived at the new land of the over-50s, to take stock and, if necessary, make a new start. One of the sporting world's ultimate role models of fitness and health, Martina Navratilova, eats no sugar, very little fat, no dairy products and drinks no alcohol, and through her 40s her energy levels and her intelligence have been stupendous. This regime may not suit everyone but you can work out what suits you. As we get older we should eat less, and better. Between the ages of 25 and 70, the average woman loses 24.2kg (11lb) of muscle, and her metabolism slows by 5 per cent every ten years after the age of 24. A 75-year-old woman needs 300 calories less per day than she did at 18, 130 less than when she was 50.

It is sensible to eat little and often, rather than to eat large meals once or twice a day. Try this out for three weeks and see if it works for you. There is a saying that the secret of a long life is to go to bed hungry (but not starving, otherwise you won't sleep well!). It's important to get enough bulk and fibre in your diet, and eat enough yoghurt to maintain the microbial population in the gut. It's best to avoid the low-nutrient sugar and fat calories of processed foods and salty snacks, and to increase dark green and orange vegetables, wholegrains and legumes, which protect us against the common diseases to which we are prone. We need an adequate intake of calcium, magnesium and vitamin D for healthy bones. We should see that our intake is sufficient of vitamins A and E, and of selenium, all anti-oxidants that protect and repair our bodies at a cellular level.

Generally speaking, moderation in all things is the golden rule. If you eat a varied diet with lots of fresh vegetables, fruits, seeds and nuts, and fish, but avoiding too many processed foods, you will be on the right track. Don't allow yourself to become obsessed with 'dieting': if you want to lose weight, change the way you eat (the word diet means 'way of daily living'), and how much, following the guidelines below. Accept the changing shape of your body as it ages, but do also recognise that weight gain is not an inevitable part of ageing, if you exercise well and eat the right food. The most important thing to recognise is that your body is your genetic inheritance and that finding the right balance of nutrition and exercise for it will give your life a comfortable balance.

The Golden Rules
- Eat breakfast: it keeps the gut in good working order and helps to keep your weight stable

Putting Some Superfoods on the Map

Carrots, sweet potatoes, cantaloupes, oranges and other red or orange vegetables or fruit contain beta-carotene, the anti-oxidant that has also been shown to be highly anti-carcinogenic.

Soya contains plant oestrogens, which protect against breast cancer, and are a valuable supplement for women of menopausal age. Drink soya milk in preference to dairy, choosing a calcium-enriched brand, and eat tofu.

Apples contain quercetin, an anti-oxidant, and lots of vitamin C. They help to keep cholesterol down, have a beneficial effect on the bowels, and improve lung capacity.

Broccoli and Brussels sprouts contain detoxifying enzymes that can block the growth of tumours. Other dark green leafy vegetables such as cabbage, kale and spring greens contain plant oestrogens too, and are a valuable source of the

powerful anti-oxidant vitamin C, and calcium.

Herrings, mackerel and sardines are rich in particular essential fatty acids, which are beneficial for the heart and are the best brain nutrients yet identified.

Garlic is powerfully anti-bacterial, limits the rise in blood cholesterol, protects against colon and stomach cancers, and heart disease.

Raw onion, shallots and leeks are also anti-bacterial, help to keep the arteries clear and contain the anti-oxidant

quercetin, which has been shown to have a role in inhibiting colon cancer.

Oat bran helps to keep cholesterol down, and oats have also been shown to have a soothing and regulating effect on the nervous system.

Olive oil, rapeseed oil and linseed oil all contain valuable essential fatty acids that are good for the skin, the body, and excellent food for the brain. Alternate them in your cooking.

Shiitake mushrooms enhance the immune system and are one of the few vegetable sources of vitamin D which determines how much calcium will be available for your metabolism, and whether to lay it down in new bone, or to soften it. They are rich in calcium and phosphorus.

Quinoa (pronounced 'keen-wa'), has significantly more protein than any other grain, and contains four times more

calcium than wheat, with extra iron, B vitamins and the valuable vitamin E.

Avocado is rich in monounsaturated oils, which have a wonderfully enriching effect on the skin. Avocados contain vitamin E (helps hot flushes), carotene, folic acid, vitamin C and potassium.

Seaweed is one of nature's richest sources of calcium and is full of minerals that help to create and maintain bone mass, to lower blood pressure and relieve menopausal symptoms.

(most overweight people skip breakfast, not realising that, deprived of food for many hours, the body thinks it's being starved and holds on to its fat reserves).

- Keep your salt and refined sugar intake low.
- Cut fats down – especially the saturated animal fats in meat and dairy produce – to 25 per cent of your daily intake (but not less than 15 per cent). They are associated with heart disease, breast and colon cancer, strokes and obesity. Choose the vegetable-based oils instead (see Superfoods, left).
- Fibre-rich foods keep blood sugar levels stable, the colon clean, and cholesterol levels down. They contain abundant vitamins and minerals and help the body to absorb them better than processed foods. So eat masses of fresh salads, vegetables, wholegrain home-made bread with low salt, fruits, nuts, seeds, pasta and cereals.
- Eating a wide variety of the right foods (see Superfoods, left) is good for the body.
- Eat organic: you take fewer industrial chemicals into the body (pesticides and fertilisers). Anyway it tastes so much better.
- Eat less (unless you are underweight), but don't get caught up in fad diets: they do not work in the long term.
- Eat live (low-fat) yoghurt to keep the digestive flora in the gut healthy.
- 'Food-combining' works wonders for the body as it ages: don't mix protein and carbohydrates at one meal, and eat fruit separately, as a snack. (All the green vegetables and salads are 'neutral' foods and can be eaten with all meals.)
- Eat fish in preference to meat: it is more nutritious and better for your brain!
- The good news: Scandinavian research has shown that 1 to 3 glasses of wine a day, combined with steady exercise, is the best combination for a long life. The resveratrol and quercetin contained in wine have a beneficial effect on the cardiovascular system.
- Drink plenty of water in between meals: filtered tap water is best, up to 2 litres (3.6 pints) per day. The body comprises two thirds water and we lose between 1 and 1½ litres (1.8-2.7 pints) per day through the skin. Water gives you energy and stamina. Drink even more when you exercise, both before and after. Too little water can:
  - dehydrate muscle leading to stiffness
  - contribute to lower-back pain
  - cause the skin to wrinkle faster
  - block up the gut leading to constipation and piles
  - cause halitosis.

What are Anti-oxidants?

Anti-oxidants are nutrients or nutrient-derived enzymes that neutralise the free radicals produced by the natural oxidation process that takes place in the human body all the time, injuring cell membranes. This process is a bit like an apple turning brown and rotting from the inside. Free radicals are also created in the body in direct response to UV light, tobacco smoke, ozone and pollutants in the atmosphere.

Chief sources of anti-oxidants are beta-carotene, found in vitamin A. Vitamins C and E are also important, with selenium close behind. Manganese, copper and zinc also play their part, so make sure that your diet contains all of these elements. If it does not, take supplements (see below).

Star Supplements

Taking a daily multivitamin pill can do no harm. If you do not eat meat, make sure that your vitamin B12 level is high enough, and remember that it is important for all women over 50 to have sufficient vitamin D, which means getting sufficient sunlight since only tiny amounts are found in food.

If you are menopausal, take the suggested herbal supplements black cohosh, agnus castus, red clover, wild yam etc. (see page 157).

- Selenium has an anti-oxidant effect, and slows down ageing.
- Gingko improves the blood supply to the brain.
- If you are not eating dairy produce, take a calcium supplement to maintain bone density.
- Magnesium is an important mineral for the not-so-young body in maintaining metabolism, healthy nerves and muscle.
- Zinc plays a part in many bodily functions, especially in maintaining skin condition, vision and sense of taste, immune system and enzyme activity.
- Fish oil supplements have been shown by Italian research trials to reduce heart-related deaths by 30 per cent.

Note: don't take supplements with tea or coffee since these can affect their absorption.

Quick recipes for healthy everyday living

To eat well and healthily without reaching for convenience foods does not have to be labour-intensive, or time-consuming, or even boring. Here are some ideas for quick, vitality-enhancing meals that balance delicious tastes with healthy ingredients.

Tell me what you eat and I will tell you what you are Brillat-Savarin (1755-1826)

Sunshine Breakfast

This delicious mixture puts a sparkle in your eye and gives you an early-morning surge of vitality.

2 tbsp organic oats

1 tbsp oat germ

1 apple, cored and grated

1 tbsp lemon juice

1 tbsp each flaked almonds and sultanas

3–4 tbsp live natural yoghurt

Honey to taste (optional)

Mix all the ingredients together in a bowl and drizzle honey over the top if desired. Eat with more yoghurt if you like.

Home-made Soya Yoghurt

Put a scant half a teaspoon of natural live yoghurt in the bottom of a plastic measuring jug. Pour 500ml (1 pint) soya milk over the

top and place the jug in a warm place such as an airing cupboard or over a boiler. Leave for up to 24 hours to set. Keep in the fridge and use within 4–5 days. It is creamy and delicious.

Simple Oats with Yoghurt

For a delightfully quick and easy breakfast, just soak organic rolled oats in milk (soya or skimmed) and allow to soak for 10 minutes. Eat with lots of plain yoghurt (soya or dairy).

Home-made Granola

Simply the best. Delicious with plain live yoghurt.
   Makes 1.5kg (3lb)

350g (12oz) oats

110g (4oz) oat bran

50g (2oz) wheatgerm

50g (2oz) coconut flakes

75g (3oz) sunflower seeds

75g (3oz) coarse oatmeal

350g (12oz) mixed nuts such as cashews, pecans, walnuts or
   almonds, cut in half

120ml (4.8fl oz) each honey and vegetable oil

1 tbsp ground cinnamon

Vanilla to flavour

   Mix all the ingredients thoroughly together in a large bowl. Turn out into two large roasting tins and bake at 170°C/325°F/gas 3 for 30 minutes, turning every 10 minutes. Allow to cool. Store in sealed containers.

Spicy Carrot Soup

This is a purée of beta-carotene, packed with anti-oxidants to make your immune system buzz. I make this soup in big batches and freeze it in yoghurt cartons (this quantity makes about nine).

Home-made granola.

or 20–25 minutes if they are large winter carrots. Add the stock cubes for the final 10 minutes of the cooking. Once they are quite tender, leave to cool a little in the liquid.

Place the cooked carrots into the blender with some of the cooking liquid and blend to a purée. Do this in batches until all the carrots are used up. Then thin out to the desired consistency – I love it really thick – with some of the remaining liquid.

Finally stir in the curry paste, to taste – I like mine hot and spicy, but this is a question of personal preference. I love to eat this soup with warm ciabatta bread and good-quality unsalted butter.

Quick Croûtons

Serves 4

3 medium slices day-old bread

4–5 tbsp olive oil

Sea salt or garlic granules to taste

Cut the crusts off the bread and cut into small dice. Drizzle the bread cubes with olive oil and toss well. Sprinkle with sea salt or garlic granules, and roast at 190°C/375°F/gas 5 for 10 minutes, tossing them from time to time, until golden and crisp.

Best Bruschettas

'In cooking, as in all the arts, simplicity is a sign of perfection,' said the Russian chef Curnonsky. And what could be simpler than chunks of toasted bread with tasty toppings, sizzled quickly under the grill?

Serves 4

1 loaf ciabatta bread

4 tbsp olive oil

4 large organic tomatoes, diced small

225g (8oz) mozzarella cheese, sliced

2 tsp dried oregano

Spicy carrot soup with quick croûtons.

Makes 2.8 litres (5 pints)

2.7kg (6lb) organic carrots

6 vegetable stock cubes

2–3 tbsp curry paste, to taste

Scrub the carrots and top and tail them. Slice lengthwise if they are big, otherwise leave them whole. This seems to give a better flavour to the soup. Cover them with water and bring to the boil. Cook, covered with a lid, for 15 minutes if they are small,

Sea salt and lots of freshly ground black pepper

Fresh basil leaves

12 black olives, pitted and chopped (optional)

1 clove garlic, crushed

Cut the bread lengthwise and then across into 8 pieces. Brush all over with olive oil. Place on a baking tray and put under a hot grill for 2–3 minutes, turning to crisp on the other side.

Mix all the other ingredients in a bowl and heap on to the toast. Drizzle with a little more olive oil, and return to the grill for another 2 minutes until bubbling. Serve hot.

Mushroom Burgers

This instant healthy meal is a far cry from a greasy beef number. My favourite bread to use for this is focaccia, otherwise any good bap-shaped bread will do.

Per person:

2 large brown mushrooms, sliced

1 large roll (preferably focaccia)

A little soft butter

Sea salt and freshly ground black pepper

A sprinkling of alfalfa sprout

3–4 rocket leaves

A few olives (optional), pitted and sliced

Either microwave the mushrooms for a couple of minutes, or grill them (if you are doing this, brush with olive oil first). Cool.

Cut the roll in half and butter lightly. Fill with the slices of mushrooms, seasoning them as you go and layering them with the alfalfa and the rocket. Close up and it is ready to eat.

Home-made Pesto Pizzas

A meal in a matter of minutes. Although it looks laughably simple, this quick fix is delicious, especially if you use fresh home-made pesto.

1 thin Italian pizza base

2–3 tbsp fresh pesto

50g (2oz) mozzarella cheese

Spread the pizza base thickly and evenly with the pesto. Cover with the mozzarella. Place on a metal baking tray and bake at 240°C/410°F/gas 8 for 10–12 minutes until the base is cooked and the cheese bubbling.

Serve with a mixed salad.

For quick and simple pesto:

Purée a large handful of basil leaves with some crushed garlic and a little sea salt and enough olive oil to work to a paste. This stores very well and you can freeze it. Usually pesto is made with pine nuts and Parmesan as well.

Puff Pastry Crust with Mediterranean Vegetables

The quickest, easiest way of making a 'pizza' invented. Elegant and light.

Serves 2

3 medium courgettes, sliced

1 tbsp olive oil (plus more to drizzle)

175g (6oz) puff pastry

2 medium tomatoes, sliced

75g (3oz) goat's cheese, crumbled

Salt and pepper

4–5 tbsp tomato passata, warmed

Roast the courgettes on a baking tray, brushed with a little oil, for 15–20 minutes at 190°C/375°F/gas 5.

Roll out the puff pastry very thinly into circles 18cm (7in) in diameter. Brush lightly with olive oil.

Arrange the slices of tomato and courgette alternately

around the puff pastry in concentric circles. Place the goat's cheese in the centre. Season with sea salt and freshly ground black pepper, and drizzle lightly with olive oil.

Bake at 220°C/425°F/gas 7 for 30–35 minutes until the pastry is well risen and the cheese melted and browned. Serve at once, with passata drizzled around the edge.

New Potatoes in Chilli Butter

You can make this with tiny young potatoes, or with older potatoes, which you dice after cooking.

Serves 4

115g (4oz) butter

1 fresh green chilli, chopped finely (de-seed if you don't like it too hot)

1kg (2.2lb) tiny new potatoes

Sea salt to taste

Fresh coriander to garnish, chopped finely

Melt the butter and add the chopped chilli. Leave to infuse for 5 minutes over a low heat, then cool.

Cook the potatoes in boiling water until tender but still slightly crunchy. Drain, and toss in the butter. Season with a little sea salt.

Serve from a warmed bowl, with fresh chopped coriander sprinkled over the top.

Broccoli with Garlic and Ginger

'It is not really an exaggeration to say that peace and happiness begin, geographically, where garlic is used in cooking,' said the great chef Boulestin. Happiness is in this case easily obtained: get cooking.

Serves 3–4

1 medium clove garlic, grated finely

2.5cm (1in) ginger, grated finely

A pinch or two of chilli powder, to taste

2 tbsp dark sesame oil

1 tbsp soy sauce

500g (1lb) broccoli

1 small bunch fresh coriander, chopped finely

Mix the garlic and ginger, and season with the chilli powder. Stir in the dark sesame oil and enough soy sauce to balance the flavours.

Steam the broccoli until quite soft, about 7–8 minutes, and leave to cool for 5–10 minutes, then cut into florets and chop the stems small. Mix into the sauce and stir thoroughly. Serve on small plates sprinkled with fresh coriander, and serve either on its own on noodles, or with fresh bread and salad.

Crushed Cauliflower with Garlic

'I hate a man who swallows his food affecting not to know what he is eating. I suspect his taste in other matters,' said Charles Lamb (1774–1834). Did you know that a cauliflower is a cabbage with a college education? According to an American saying, it is. Well, just shows what an education can do for you.

Serves 2

2 tbsp butter

1 large clove garlic, chopped very finely

1 medium cauliflower, steamed until soft

Sea salt to taste

Melt the butter and stir in the garlic. Cook until softened over a gentle heat, about 3 minutes. Then turn up the heat and add the cauliflower. Crush it as it warms through, using a potato masher. This will take about 5 minutes. Season to taste with a tiny amount of sea salt, and brown it very lightly under a hot grill before serving.

Salad of Grilled Vegetables with Herbs

Delicious light food which looks wonderful and smells aromatic, this easy salad makes a perfect lunch or supper dish, served with fresh bread.

Serves 4

For the dressing:

4 tbsp balsamic vinegar

2 tbsp water

6 tbsp extra virgin olive oil

Sea salt and freshly ground black pepper

Mix the vinegar with the water. Add the oil, whisk well and season with sea salt and freshly ground black pepper.

For the grilled vegetables:

1 small aubergine, cut in half lengthwise and then into thin diagonal slices

1 yellow pepper, halved, de-seeded and cut into wide strips

2 large courgettes, sliced diagonally about 5mm (1/4in) thick

4 medium flat mushrooms, sliced thickly

Olive oil

Toss the vegetables in enough oil to coat them lightly. Place under a hot grill for 2–3 minutes each side, or until they brown slightly and soften. Cool.

For the herb salad:

Salad leaves

12 mint leaves, shredded

8 basil leaves, torn

2 large shallots, chopped finely

Arrange the vegetables around the edge of 4 plates. Toss the salad with the herbs, shallots and vinaigrette and pile into the centre of the plate.

Green Salad with Goat's Cheese Vinaigrette

This goat's cheese dressing transforms a simple salad and makes it a snack in itself served with warm crusty bread. I love to use rocket leaves, sometimes mixed with lamb's lettuce, but a variety of salad leaves is lovely too.

Serves 2

For the vinaigrette:

2 tbsp water

1$^{1}/_{2}$ tbsp lemon juice

2$^{1}/_{2}$ tbsp olive oil

Lots of freshly ground black pepper

50g (2oz) goat's cheese

Put all the ingredients into a small blender and work until completely smooth. Leave to stand.

For the salad:

Large amounts (to taste!) of the following:

Lamb's lettuce

Rocket leaves

Soft lettuce leaves of many colours

Radicchio

Croûtons (see page 142)

Toss the leaves in the dressing just before serving, and sprinkle with croûtons.

Salad of Feta and Garlic Couscous with Broccoli

This brilliant salad looks as lovely as it tastes, and makes a delicious lunch or simple supper dish, served with a leafy salad and crusty bread.

Serves 4

Feta and garlic couscous with broccoli.

1 clove garlic, crushed

1¹/₂ tbsp olive oil

75g (3oz) couscous, cooked according to the instructions

Sea salt and freshly ground black pepper

115g (4oz) feta cheese, cubed

1 large ripe avocado, peeled and diced small

225g (8oz) broccoli florets, cooked until soft

50g (2oz) olives (optional), pitted and halved

Crush the garlic into the oil and leave to stand for several minutes. Drain off any excess water from the couscous and mix with the garlic oil. Season thoroughly with sea salt and freshly ground black pepper.

Fold in the cheese, diced avocado and broccoli florets gently. Decorate with the olives, if using. Serve at room temperature.

Amaretti Fruit Crumble

This delicate crumble with its nuance of almond in the flavour is delicious served with yoghurt, or with old-fashioned custard.

Serves 6–8

100g (3¹/₂oz) butter

225g (8oz) self-raising flour, sifted

50g (2oz) caster sugar

175g (6oz) amaretti biscuits, crushed

750g (1¹/₂lb) fruit such as pears, apples, blueberries – or a combination, washed

50g (2oz) caster sugar

Rub the butter into the flour. Stir in the sugar and fold in the amaretti crumbs.

Slice the pears or apples thinly, leaving their skins on. Place in a large, shallow baking dish and toss in the sugar. Sprinkle the crumble over the top and press down with the back of a fork.

Bake at the bottom of the oven set at 190°C/375°F/gas 5, for 40 minutes. Cool a little, and serve hot or warm.

Summer Melon Medley

A mouth-watering dessert, ideal for a special occasion in summer.

Serves 4–6

1 each galia, honeydew and charentais melons

1 large slice watermelon

125g (4oz) icing sugar

225g (8oz) blueberries, sliced

optional extra fruit such as lychees, seedless grapes, mango

Juice of 1 lime

Optional vodka (about 3 tbsp)

Mint leaves for decoration

De-seed the melons and scoop the flesh into balls. Cut the watermelon into small chunks, removing as many seeds as possible. Sift the sugar over the melon, blueberries and optional fruit if using and toss well. Add the lime juice and optional vodka. Chill for 2 hours and decorate with mint leaves.

Fruit Skewers

These are delicious barbecued, but also mouth-watering fresh from the grill.

Serves 4

150ml (¹/4 pint) sake or dry sherry or white wine

50g (2oz) caster sugar

2 star anise

¹/2 tsp five-spice powder

750g (1¹/2lb) mixed fruits such as seedless grapes, lychees, mango, pineapple, banana, pear

Place the wine, sugar and star anise in a small saucepan and heat until the sugar dissolves. Bring to the boil and boil rapidly for 2 minutes. Stir in the five-spice powder.

Prepare the fruit by cutting into bite-size cubes. Thread on to skewers. Put on to a shallow plate and pour the syrup over them. Allow to marinate for at least an hour.

Cook under a preheated grill on a baking tray lined with foil, turning occasionally until they are lightly browned. Serve immediately with cream.

Summer melon medley.

menopause: a self-help guide

menopause: a self-help guide

The truth is that fewer women come to grief at this obstacle than at any other in their tempestuous lives, though it is one of the stiffest challenges they ever face Germaine Greer

What is the menopause?

Menopause is a natural life event that has many advantages and freedoms. It attracts negative attitudes because it is not well understood, and although a minority of women experience deep discomfort, most do not, at least for any length of time, and those who do can do much to help themselves. Lifestyle, nutrition and exercise are vital strategies effective in maintaining the health and balance of the body in middle and older age.

Menopause means the end of menstruation, the end of periods, the end of monthly bleeding. It is also known as 'the change', and the transition time during and after menopause is often termed 'the climacteric'. Menopause is accompanied by changes in hormone levels: hormones are body chemicals that control cell chemistry. They are produced by the various glands that affect metabolism, hair distribution, mental and emotional states, the immune system, your chances of getting osteoporosis, heart disease, and the way in which you age.

At menopause, your levels of progesterone fall dramatically, even to zero, while oestrogen levels are maintained but at a much lower rate than before. Body fat helps to produce this oestrogen. The adrenal glands start to produce a type of female hormone to accompany the diminishing levels of oestrogen produced by the ovaries. The usual test for assessing hormone levels is the follicle-stimulating hormone (FSH) test, which is done by a doctor. There is also a blood oestrogen test, and a DIY kit for a saliva test. If you are concerned about osteoporosis, ask your doctor to arrange a bone density scan.

We all start life with a finite number of egg cells, and gradually run out of them between the ages of 44 and 55 (smokers tend to experience menopause up to two years earlier than non-smokers). Only a few eggs remain by the time of the menopause. Just before its onset, although periods may still be regular, the first symptoms – hot flushes and mood swings – may appear. At the second stage, ovary function declines, periods become irregular, and symptoms may become more severe. From your last period onwards, usually between the ages of 51 and 55, you have reached menopause (officially, when you have had no period for a year).

Hormones affect us on both physical and mental levels, and lack of hormones likewise. They impact on breast tissue, body hair and physical shape as well as emotional and psychological balance. Swings in confidence, self-esteem, mood and outlook are commonly experienced as part of the monthly cycle, and at menopause these may become more dominant for a while until the body adjusts to a new balance in body chemistry. The most important thing is to view this positively, and to understand the process, rather than thinking of it as a disease, a deficiency, or a failure of the body to function 'properly'. The body is learning to function in a *different* way, and there are many things that you can do to help it.

The menopause is a symbolic change as well as a chemical one. The transition from fertility to infertility may be empowering for some, while for others it may lower their sense of self-worth and status. In cultures where youth is venerated, it may be accompanied by the fear of diminishing beauty and sexual attractiveness. These prevailing stereotypes make us feel uncomfortable with ourselves if they are accepted uncritically. Rather than being influenced by them we need to nurture the psychological confidence that comes from learning to understand ourselves better (see page 74). Maybe it is OK to be older, look older, behave older. We all know older women who are truly beautiful in the acceptance of their age. Mutton dressed up as lamb never was that pretty.

Symptoms

You may experience some of the symptoms listed below before and during menopause, although they may not be related to menopause at all, but to the natural process of ageing which affects men just as much as women. As it stands, it makes a frightening list: but do remember that the symptoms vary greatly in intensity and duration. In fact, you may experience none of them, or just a few mild ones. It's only if you are seriously unlucky that you'll have them all! Surveys have shown that less than one quarter of all women find their symptoms problematical. If you do, console yourself with the knowledge that they are short-lived, and there are things that you can do about them:

- hot flushes, or flashes (known also as 'power-surges')
- night sweats
- heart palpitations
- dizziness
- headaches
- itchy skin
- loss of concentration or memory
- irritability
- change in sleep patterns
- vaginal dryness
- loss of libido
- cystitis
- incontinence
- dry skin
- thinning skin
- broken capillaries or discolouration
- weight gain
- change in hair quality
- lack of energy
- depression
- anxiety
- rapid mood changes
- low self-confidence
- panic attacks
- osteoporosis

How to Deal with the Symptoms

Taking responsibility for your own health is the first step towards coping well with the menopause.

- In general: take up exercise, control your weight, and follow the guidelines for foods on page 165. Drink plenty of water, consider taking supplements (see page 158), and reduce your stress levels.
- Use a vaginal lubricant if dryness is disrupting your sex life (see page 94).
- Consider therapies such as aromatherapy to help you relax and balance yourself.
- Alternative medicine can help your transition through menopause: homeopathy, acupuncture, herbal medicine, nutritional therapy and naturopathy can all help.
- Practise the 'yoga for menopause' exercises on page 162.
- Consider the pros and cons of HRT (see page 154) and weigh them up.
- Wear cotton rather than man-made fibres if you are suffering from sweats and hot flushes. Likewise use linen or cotton for your bed covers.
- Wear thin layers of clothing so that you can peel them off to cool down when you need to.
- Take plenty of cool baths and use anti-perspirant afterwards.
- Avoid hot drinks and spicy foods, especially at night before going to bed.
- Reduce your intake of animal protein.
- Include natural plant oestrogens in your diet (see page 138).

- Eat less: your body needs less fuel than it used to. You may need to reduce your daily intake by as much as 300 calories.
- Alcohol, caffeine and smoking may worsen your symptoms, so avoid them.
- Don't eat too much too late: you may sleep less well on a full stomach.
- Drink herbal teas with melissa and lemon.
- Learn deep-breathing techniques to help with hot flushes (see page 136).
- Take up a new interest that you enjoy and that stimulates you mentally.
- Consult your doctor if there is a history of osteoporosis in your family.

HRT

Hormone Replacement Therapy (HRT) supplies the female body with hormones when its own production slows down. It alleviates or prevents the symptoms of menopause (see page 152) by restoring the levels of oestrogen or progesterone or both. It is claimed by some as a panacea for all ills, from an ageing skin to osteoporosis, and as a protection against heart disease. However, like anything else it has its pros and cons: it is a synthesised drug, a pharmaceutical product. Some people gain weight on HRT, others experience uncomfortable side effects. You have to make your own personal decision about whether or for how long to use it, based on your fitness level, personal needs, family history, and on an educated look at what its effects are likely to be on your health.

The Pros

- It reduces the risk of bone fracture, especially spine, hip and wrist, by possibly 70 per cent.
- It protects against coronary heart disease which is a major cause of death in older women, so if you have a family history of this condition it is worth consulting with your doctor.
- It's believed to reduce the risk and intensity of Alzheimer's disease.
- It relieves hot flushes, vaginal dryness and other menopausal symptoms (see page 152).
- It lessens the likelihood of problems with concentration and memory, and is said to enable women to stay mentally alert for longer.

The Cons

- HRT increases the risk of breast and womb cancer.
- It may increase the risk of raised blood pressure, stroke and thrombosis.
- Monthly periods continue (on most forms of HRT).
- One of the most popular forms of HRT is extracted from the urine of pregnant mares and raises genuine animal welfare concerns.
- It may cause mood swings, weight gain, depression, water retention and headaches.
- Initial short-term effects may include breast tenderness, irregular bleeding, deep-vein thrombosis, leg cramps, hair loss and nausea.

Types of HRT

There are around 30 types of HRT available on prescription, so consult your doctor as to the form that might suit you best. They include:

- monthly bleed tablets
- 3-monthly bleed tablets
- period-free HRT
- vaginal preparations (creams and pessaries)
- skin patch or gel
- implant

'Natural' Progesterone

Progesterone creams are currently hyped as a 'natural alternative' to HRT. They are not, however, 'natural', they are a synthesised form of soya (originally it was wild yam), processed in a laboratory, and contain powerful pharmaceutical agents. Claims are made that progesterone is the 'fountain of youth', but although some women find it beneficial, others experience uncomfortable side-effects and even a loss in bone density. Some researchers claim that progesterone is not absorbed through the skin – in which case this cream is nothing more than an expensive placebo. The effects of its long-term use are not yet established so when considering whether to use it as a treatment, it's worth weighing up the risks and/or looking at other options.

What to Discuss with Your Doctor

- Discuss your family history or personal medical history, especially if that includes heart disease, or breast or womb cancers.
- Seek advice if you have high blood pressure,

fibroids, or suffer from migraines, or liver or kidney disease.

Questions to Ask Your Doctor

- What are the long-term health risks?
- What are the side-effects likely to be?
- How often should I have HRT check-ups?
- How long should I take it for?
- How often will I need to have mammograms and cervical smears?
- What are the alternatives to consider?

Natural alternatives to HRT

Nutrition

Good nutrition during the menopause can help your body significantly in making the inevitable adjustments. You can keep your hormones balanced, your energy levels stable, and menopausal symptoms at a minimum, if you follow the basic guidelines below:

DO

- Accept the fact that you may have to work at staying healthy. You may need to make quite a few drastic changes in your habits both in how you eat and in the exercise you take.
- Eat foods with vitamin D in them such as oily fish, butter, egg yolks, liver and milk (calcium-fortified if necessary).

- Keep your blood sugar levels stable by reducing your intake of refined foods and making sure that about half your calorie intake comes from complex carbohydrates (grains, beans and root vegetables) and fruit.
- Get enough of the right essential fatty acids by eating cold-pressed oils, especially linseed, and extra-virgin olive oil, organic butter in moderation, nuts and seeds, tahini, oily fish and unhydrogenated margarines.
- Eat lots of natural fibre in vegetables and grains, and avoid large amounts of bran since it impedes calcium absorption.
- Eat calcium-rich foods such as wholemeal cereals, pulses, dried fruit, canned salmon and sardines (eat the bones), fresh salmon, dark green leafy vegetables like spinach, kale and broccoli, calcium-fortified soya, yoghurt and whole milk.
- Eat a healthy breakfast. Oats are an ideal food.
- Eat fish rather than meat.
- Eat small, frequent meals rather than leaving long gaps between eating. Stay in shape by eating the right foods in the right amounts! If you need to shed weight, just eat half your usual quantities at every meal (most of us eat too much anyway).
- Try food-combining, which means not mixing protein and carbohydrate at the same meal, and eating fruit separately, as a snack (see page 139).
- Eat soy-based foods that contain phyto-oestrogens, which the body converts into hormone-like substances. Soya contains two flavonoid compounds that have mild oestrogenic activity. Japanese women have minimal menopausal problems and this may be due to the large amounts of soya in their diet. Other useful plant sources include linseed and flaxseed oils, oats, corn, barley, millet, buckwheat, wild rice, soya flour, flax oil, green vegetables, and pulses.
- Eat alkaline foods known to protect bone density: sprouted seeds, yoghurt, almonds, Brazil nuts and buckwheat for example.
- Drink plenty of mineral or filtered water.
- Fast from time to time: an occasional day on nothing but water or herbal teas flushes toxins out of the system.

DON'T
- Smoke. Smoking lowers blood oestrogen levels and can trigger early menopause.
- Indulge in sugar, coffee, tea, alcohol and salt: they do not help hot flushes. Alcohol burns off the small supply of oestrogen present in the body at menopause and interferes with calcium metabolism. Salt leaches calcium from the bones, and caffeine causes calcium to be excreted. It is diuretic and flushes vital nutrients and trace elements out of the body.
- Overdo the bacon and eggs. Animal proteins are acid-forming and the body neutralises them by using its sodium and calcium supply, and the latter is taken from the bones.
- Overdo cholesterol and dairy foods. Switch to soya products (see above).
- Use aluminium pans: aluminium leaches into the

water and impedes the metabolism of calcium. Use glass, enamel or stainless steel instead.

- Use unblended vegetable oils, for preference cold-pressed (which means unprocessed). Avoid palm oil – it is a saturated fat made from the coconut palm.
- Eat processed foods: they contain high amounts of refined carbohydrates and sodium. (See also 'Superfoods for the Menopause', page 165.)

Herbs

Herbs are powerful medicines, and have been used worldwide for centuries. Tibetan and Chinese herbal medicine is becoming increasingly acknowledged by the West which has largely replaced its herbal lore with pharmaceuticals – although many modern drugs are a synthesised form of plant remedies. Certain herbs have a balancing effect on the body's hormones and allow the body to restore itself to full function in a natural way. It is usually best to take a mixture, and good ready-made herbal preparations designed to help women at the menopause are available. You can take them either in tincture form (about 1 teaspoon in water 3 times a day) or in capsule form. As the herbs rebalance your hormones you reduce the amounts and gradually find that you don't need them any more. Rather than just alleviating symptoms, herbs cure them. Consult a herbalist to make sure that you take them in the correct amounts. Look out for:

Black cohosh *(Cimicifuga racemosa)* helps painful periods, re-establishes hormone balance, reduces hot flushes and water retention.

Agnus castus *(Vitex/chasteberry)* stimulates the pituitary gland, which controls the balance of hormones in the body. It restores balance where there is deficit or excess, it helps to regulate periods, helps with heavy bleeding and PMT, reduces hot flushes and balances oestrogen levels.

Wild yam *(Dioscorea villosa)* is anti-spasmodic and can help to relieve painful periods. It appears that the disogenin in wild yam can imitate the effects of oestrogen in our bodies. It works as a balancer if there is deficiency or excess.

Dong quai *(Radix angelica sinensis)* is used extensively in Chinese medicine, for alleviating period pain, reducing hot flushes and night sweats and alleviating vaginal dryness. It is the most frequently used herb for menstrual complaints.

Motherwort *(Leonurus cardiaca)* has been used for centuries. It alleviates painful periods and hot flushes, it's calming and helps to combat insomnia, and it restores elasticity and thickness to the vaginal walls, lessening vaginal dryness.

Dandelion *(Taraxacum officinalis)* cleanses and detoxes the liver, and is a powerful diuretic so helps reduce water retention.

Yarrow *(Achillea millefolium)* alleviates hot flushes, and helps with heavy bleeding and painful periods.

False Unicorn Root *(Chamaelirium luteum)* has a balancing effect on the hormones and is a tonic for the reproductive system.

Other herbs that help regulate the body chemistry in menopause are liquorice, red clover, evening primrose and St John's Wort, which alleviates mood swings. Gingko, ginger and garlic protect the heart from disease, and ginseng (*Panax spp.*) is a powerful remedy for many menopausal symptoms, such as vaginal dryness, hot flushes and sweats, anxiety and tension, and palpitations. It is an 'adaptogen' which both tranquillises and energises the system (this herb is not, however, for the hyperactive or the agitated, but rather for those who feel fatigue during the climacteric).

Supplements

The following daily supplements may be helpful during the menopause:

- a good multivitamin, with evening primrose added, plus boron
- 15mg zinc citrate
- combined magnesium/calcium with a ratio of 2:1
- 50mg vitamin B complex
- 1000mg linseed oil
- extra vitamin D and E

Aromatherapy

Pure essential plant oils have a healing effect and are extracted from the flowers, leaves, bark, stem, seeds and peel of particular plants. They usually smell lovely, and are absorbed into the bloodstream through the skin and lungs. They are powerful and should be used judiciously, whether through a massage from a qualified aromatherapist, a few drops in a bath, footbath or shower, via inhalation

Certain supplements are helpful at menopause.

over hot water, mixed into a base oil or using a vaporiser. The most valuable oils at menopause are frankincense, lavender, camomile, geranium, rose, jasmine, neroli, ylang-ylang, bergamot, sandalwood and clary sage.

Acupuncture

Acupuncture is the time-honoured oriental technique of inserting fine needles, quite painlessly, into the meridians or energy channels of the body in order to balance energies. Treatments heal many conditions and help the body to restore itself to full vitality. A skilled acupuncturist may be able to correct hormone and energy imbalances. Go by recommendation, or contact a national organisation for local contacts.

Homeopathy

This increasingly popular – and very safe – form of alternative medicine helps the body to balance itself. Tiny amounts of natural substances in solution are used to cure a wide range of complaints, and work as well on animals as they do on humans. The principle behind homeopathy is 'like cures like'. A homeopath takes a detailed history so that your remedies are tailored to you personally. A number of remedies have been shown to help menopausal women. Consult a qualified homeopath who has been recommended to you, or, failing that, to contact a national organisation for a local practitioner.

Lavender oil is beautifully relaxing.

Exercise at the menopause

The importance of regular exercise before and during the menopause cannot be over-emphasised. No matter how much you would prefer not to do it, exercise does make you feel better. It regulates physiological and mental balance, and because it releases endorphins into the bloodstream, it alleviates stress, reduces anxiety and makes you feel more relaxed and at one with yourself. It can relieve specific menopausal symptoms (see page 152), it blows away the clouds in the mind, it reduces appetite, helps to make you hungry for the right things, and keeps your bone density at healthy levels. Just two hours of brisk walking per week, or one hour at the gym will help to keep your bones in good condition. It's a good investment of your time! I do one session a week at the gym and often have to force myself to get there, but invariably I feel a million times better afterwards, invigorated and positive.

Exercise, paradoxically, is energising: you might think that expending energy depletes you but it doesn't, it revitalises. Of course, different forms of exercise have different benefits: aerobic work strengthens the heart and lungs; yoga relaxes you as well as toning muscles, stretching you and keeping you supple well into old age; weight-bearing exercise like brisk walking, running and yoga, too, can help to keep osteoporosis at bay. Exercise boosts your metabolism, helps you sleep better, improves your lymphatic flow and keeps blood sugar levels

steady. Specifically useful at menopause is the effect that it has on the adrenal glands: it keeps them healthy and stimulated, which is important since they convert androstenadione to oestrone which is the body's chief source of oestrogen at the menopause.

All that being said, don't go mad either. Too *much* exercise can be bad for you. Personally, I love to walk, to enjoy the fresh air and the changing seasons, and I find that the soothing effect it has on the mind and the emotions is as valuable to me as the physical benefits.

Best Forms of Exercise for the Menopause

In moderation (see page 119), the following are safe, gentle forms of exercise that involve weight bearing and help to prevent osteoporosis: brisk walking, jogging, rebounding, racket sports, dancing, yoga and cycling.

Controlling weight at the menopause

Body weight may fluctuate around the menopause as your hormones establish a new balance. Body fat acts as a manufacturing plant for oestrogen, and we need a minimum of 25 per cent fat to keep this function intact. This does not mean we have to put on weight; it may mean a different distribution of weight and a slight change in shape. But if you are eating the right things and taking sensible amounts of exercise, this may not be noticeable to anyone but you. Emotional factors around this time are more likely to disrupt your regular weight than physiological ones. If you understand what is happening, you are in a stronger position to deal with the situation in the best way for you. This may mean taking more exercise, making changes in your work life, transforming your relationships, or understanding your own personality to move through this period of change, with the help of a counsellor, priest or friend.

On a purely physical level, it is possible to eat more and weigh less. If you eat a higher proportion of carbohydrate in your diet and cut right down on added sugar – those empty calories in refined and processed foods, and alcohol – excess weight may fall off. But do make sure that you get the right amount of essential fatty acids (see page 137), otherwise your skin and brain cells will suffer! Taking zinc as a supplement may help too – zinc controls appetite, whereas a deficiency makes us crave foods. Chromium controls levels of fat and cholesterol in the blood, and vitamin C both lowers cholesterol, and converts glucose to energy.

Always eat breakfast: most people who are overweight don't (see page 137). Eat slowly and savour your food. Above all control your thinking about food. Thinking about food triggers the brain to activate a physiological response: saliva flows, the gastric juices wake up, and you think you're hungry. You may not actually *need* food but your body makes you feel as if you do. If this happens, drink a large glass of water instead (the body often confuses thirst with hunger and most of us don't drink anything like enough). Bear in mind that we are made up of nearly 80 per cent water. Cells are being replaced all the time, so we need it as a nutrient! Thinking 'I'm not hungry' goes a long way to controlling our food intake if it is a problem. The body always follows the brain: train yourself to think differently.

We may have a habit of using food as compensation or reward, and come to associate it with feeling good about ourselves. Do yourself a favour and untie that knot. Food is beautiful and it makes you feel good if you eat when you're hungry, but not for reasons of emotional manipulation, which in any case are hollow since this habit does not deliver what it appears to promise. Food for the wrong reasons can make you feel guilty and ashamed and fat. Getting your mind around that, and training yourself to have a healthy attitude to food, will help you enjoy it all the more. Find out what triggers your desire to eat, and when that trigger triggers, take control.

Perhaps you are eating too much because you crave nourishment of another kind. Perhaps an intellectual challenge will meet that need. Simply learning a new language or studying a subject you've always been interested in will be sufficient to break the habit of reaching for the biscuits or overeating at mealtimes. Or maybe you are bored, and need to become more involved with other people in a community activity or other kind of work. Or there may be a hunger less easy to define in your life that you are seeking to satisfy, which

Menopause exercises

This series of yoga asanas is designed for women of a certain age to balance energy, strengthen bone density, maintain suppleness, and induce relaxation.

1. Take legs very wide, feet straight, stretch trunk down, head towards floor, bending elbows, breathe

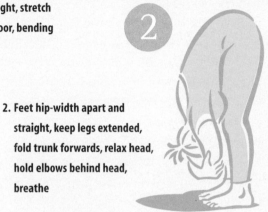

2. Feet hip-width apart and straight, keep legs extended, fold trunk forwards, relax head, hold elbows behind head, breathe

3. Kneel, place hands shoulder-width apart and straight on floor, lift hips, adjust feet to hip-width apart and straight, stretch trunk keeping shoulders soft, breathe

4. Sit, one leg stretched in front, other leg bent to side, heel to groin, stretch forwards over extended leg, arms forward, relax head, breathe

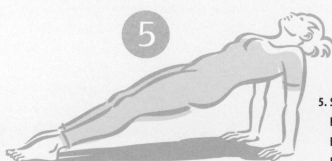

5. Sit with knees up, feet to floor, take arms behind body, hands facing towards feet, lift hips to bring body into diagonal line, look up, breathe

6

6. Headstand is for advanced yoga practitioners ONLY. Beginners, only ever do this with a teacher

7

7. Sit with legs fully extended, lean back on to elbows, arch back and bring top of head to floor, fold arms behind head keeping back arched, breathe

8

8. Stretch both legs out in front, fold at the hips and stretch forwards, relax head down, hands resting beside legs on floor

9

9. Shoulderstand
NB! This should be done only by experienced practitioners or under instruction from a teacher

10

10. Plough
NB! This should be done only by experienced practitioners or under instruction from a teacher

11

11. Sit with soles of feet together, knees dropped to side, lie back on a bolster, tuck chin down slightly to release neck, relax shoulders and arms, close eyes, soften the face, breathe, relax completely. Use eye bag on page 104 for all resting positions.

may be resolved by new relationships or by taking up a spiritual practice.

Changing established habits, like when and how you eat, and how much (eat less), and how often you open the fridge door, can help you to become more aware of your behaviour around food. Keeping a food diary may help. If you think you feel hungry, distract yourself, find something else interesting to do, or grab that glass of water! It may actually be that you are tired and need to rest rather than eat. Eat when hungry, goes a Zen saying, rest when tired. It doesn't matter when! Eat little and often (and well, so that you really enjoy it) rather than leaving food for a long time until blood sugar levels drop making you so desperate that you are likely to grab the wrong food – and too much of it – just to give you an energy rush.

Eating well and 'sensibly' does not mean no fun. Give yourself treats from time to time, but just don't get hooked on them. The occasional patisserie or chocolate is not going to make any difference at all to your health or your waistline. Forbidden fruit is all the more delicious for not being stolen very often!

Sex and the menopause

There are three schools of thought here: one, that you are past it, on the scrapheap and no longer attractive enough for sex; two, that you have lost your libido anyway; three, that you have a surge of testosterone and are a public menace. These extremes of thinking may not apply to you, but there may be changes in your sex life around this time, and it is as well to take stock of them. Take charge of your life and direct the way you want it to go.

It's simply untrue to say that the menopause makes you less attractive. Other things may do but don't blame it all on your hormones. Look at other parts of your life: if your self-esteem is low (number one) this may be linked to your work, your family or other relationships, to boredom, to being too heavy or not taking enough exercise. Add your own reasons to this list. Older women who have vitality, are interested, interesting, and relatively physically fit, are beautiful women. All that attraction stuff comes from inside, it's nothing to do with wonderful skins, firm buttocks, pert cleavages and perfect hair. These attributes may induce lust, but beauty is something else and that's what is attractive in older age. Don't let the advertisements about fountains of eternal youth fool you: mutton cosmetically disguised as lamb is repellent.

If you *do* have an active and happy sex life, and if you are one of those women whose levels of testosterone rise at menopause, making you feel sexually alive, assertive and motivated, there are things to bear in mind. You may suffer from vaginal dryness, in which case apply an oestrogen gel available over the counter to lubricate the vagina. Take more vitamin E to keep your skin supple. Wait for one full period-free year before abandoning contraception (two years if you are

Superfoods for the menopause

Research is changing all the time so find out what works for your body, and what makes you feel healthy, but try to include the following in your diet, in a balance that suits you:

- fresh organic fruit
- organic dried fruits, sulphur dioxide-free
- fresh organic vegetables
- whole grains: rice (both brown and white), oats, couscous, bulghar wheat, buckwheat, millet and barley
- breakfast mueslis, organic and sugar-free

- organic breads, wholemeal and whole-wheat, breads using unbleached flour
- pasta both white and wholemeal, buckwheat noodles, rice noodles
- nuts and seeds
- beans and pulses of all kinds
- fish, especially the oily fish such as mackerel, tuna, salmon and sardines, but also cod, trout and plaice etc.
- organic free-range eggs
- soya milk (calcium-enriched) or rice milk, oat milk instead of dairy

- yoghurt (you can make your own soya yoghurt – see page 140)
- cold-pressed oils (linseed, flax, safflower, sunflower, sesame), extra-virgin olive oil, unhydrogenated margarines, a little organic butter
- herb teas, unsweetened fruit juices, filtered water
- ginger, garlic, herbs, lemon, soy sauce
- a little free-range organic meat, a few convenience foods and occasional treats of biscuits, cakes, desserts

under 50 when the menopause kicks in). Enjoy your post-menopausal zest! Sex can be great therapy even when you're a bit saggy and wrinkly (chances are he is too). Research shows that people with a satisfying sex life are physically healthier as well as being more relaxed. Sex releases tension, calms you, boosts the immune system, and releases endorphins giving you that feel-good glow. It can be a great healer.

Alternatively you may well experience loss of libido around menopause. If this causes a problem in your relationship, then you will need to deal with this (see Love Is All There Is, page 88), but it may not do. After all, some men lose libido too. It may come as quite a relief to both of you to let up on your sex life, and to find other ways of becoming close (see page 91). People are not happy to admit this, but boredom is a huge factor in diminishing libido: sex is sex, and unless you are into kinky sex it's a pretty limited occupation, particularly with the same partner. Sex with the same person for years on end can be boring and pointless. How many of us, truthfully, have had to lie back and put up with it while he gets his rocks off? Sex is not always about loving and relationship (albeit lovely when it is), it's often about needs as basic as the need to sneeze. Talk about it with your partner: keep communication lines open.

Society is so obsessed with everything sexual that we feel a cultural pressure to have what is called a 'healthy sex life' and we imagine that everyone else is having it off every other minute.

We imagine that if we 'work at it' i.e. try out absurd new techniques and positions, that we will regain the sexual passion of yesteryear. Perhaps that's true for some, but it may not be for everyone. Couples don't talk about it enough between themselves, not frankly at any rate. Perhaps it *is* OK to have less sex as we grow older, perhaps we *can* admit that it feels really good to abstain. It is not a failure. Germaine Greer, in her inspiring and often funny book *The Change* writes, 'Some women, the lucky ones I shall argue, lose interest in sex after the menopause.' Permission to elect for a celibate period in your life.

There is freedom around celibacy, it clears relationships of complications and hooks and power struggles and manipulation. It is amazingly empowering and can change the way in which you relate to the opposite gender. You can be far more open with them and meet them on different ground. You may choose to rest from your sexual activity for a while – and then suddenly life may present you with a new situation in which your soul blossoms into a late-flowering love, and then you might decide to include sex as part of the relationship. Or not. A friend of mine, a 90-year-old poet, told me that when she was 75 she fell passionately in love with a musician who was in his mid-30s. They had a powerful affair – probably unconsummated (she was too old-fashioned to talk about explicit details) but certainly deeply loving with a great deal of physical contact which meant the world to both of them. She would look at her veined and wrinkled hand on his younger skin, and laugh ruefully at the absurdity of human love in all its inevitability and its power to transform us.

Osteoporosis: the facts

You probably think of your skeleton as being something solid, permanent and unchanging, but bones are just as alive as other body tissue. Bones change all the time, they absorb and excrete, they heal when damaged. Our bones account for 10-15 per cent of our body weight, and their mineral content is formed of calcium. Vitamin D controls the calcium and phosphorus level in the bones. As we age, we absorb calcium less easily and our bones become 'thinner', so in order to prevent excessive bone loss we need to maintain our bone health. Osteoporosis means, literally, porous bones, and it affects one in three women during their lifetime. The inner tissue structure of bone is formed like honeycomb, with blood vessels and bone marrow in the spaces, and as these spaces become bigger, as happens in osteoporosis, the bone becomes fragile and more likely to snap. It becomes so porous that falling, however lightly, can break a bone – most commonly in the wrist, spine or hip.

The marked decrease of calcium absorption in older women is aggravated by menopause and sometimes by inadequate exposure to regular sunlight. Added to this, bone loss is part of the natural ageing process. When the ovaries cease producing oestrogen, or when you over-exercise or under-eat, or have a hysterectomy, this loss is accelerated and you are at risk of osteoporosis unless you take measures to look after your bone health. There are several things you can do to ensure that you are less at risk of 'brittle bones' as you grow older, and none of them is difficult.

Risk Factors
- Lack of exercise
- Long-term immobility
- Poor diet, low in calcium
- Low body weight (underweight for your height and frame)
- Heavy drinking: more than three units per day
- Smoking
- Early menopause (before 45)
- Early hysterectomy (before 45)
- Long-term use of corticosteroids
- Family history of osteoporosis
- Malabsorption problems (Coeliac disease, Crohn's disease, gastric surgery)

Reducing Bone Loss
- Eat a bone-friendly diet that includes calcium (see page 165). One of the best sources is milk: 500ml (1 pint) contains 750mg calcium, and skimmed milk is slightly higher than whole milk. Low-fat yoghurt, cheese, spinach, Brazil nuts and tofu (which has the highest content of any of these) are also good sources.

- Take regular weight-bearing exercise such as brisk walking, jogging, tennis, yoga (see page 125).
- Give up smoking. Today.
- Take a vitamin D supplement (800iu per day), and get outdoors (but don't over expose to sunshine because of the risk of skin cancer).
- Take a calcium (1000mg per day) supplement.
- Limit your alcohol intake to 21 units per week. A unit is equivalent to a small glass of wine, a measure of spirits or half a pint of beer or cider, so this is no hardship; in fact it is currently considered that a couple of glasses of wine per day are good for your bone health. Oh good.

Preventing Bone Loss

Consult your doctor about undergoing any of the following treatments: HRT (see pages 154–5); bisphosphonates (consult your doctor); Selective Estrogen Receptor Modulators e.g. raloxifene (trade name 'Evista').

Testing For Osteoporosis

A bone density scan is used to measure the porosity of bones. It is a simple procedure that uses very low doses of radiation – less than you are exposed to walking down the average city street. You lie on a bench while the machine scans your spine and hips, and the data collected can diagnose osteoporosis (or lack of), assess your risk of fracturing, and monitor the effects of treatment

if you need it. Your doctor will assess whether you need a scan and can refer you.

Urine tests can also measure bone breakdown, and ultrasound is sometimes used to build up electronic images of bone structure and mass but cannot as yet be used to diagnose osteoporosis.

money
matters

money matters

The greater part of our happiness or misery depends on our dispositions and not on our circumstances Martha Washington

It is worth bearing in mind the above words when struggling to make sense of our finances, especially for those who are single in their later years as many women are. Divorce or widowhood after 50 can present major financial problems for women, especially if they have been dependent on their men as the wage earner. It is useful to review and prioritise values when financial complications arise: if our priorities are safely rooted somewhere other than in the bank, money issues will become less threatening than they might at first appear. Financial hazards can arise at any stage of life. A friend of mine in her early 50s fell in love with a man who turned out to be a carpetbagger. He used up all her savings and forced her to move out of her beloved home into a much smaller place because he was unable to pay the mortgage. Don't

always leave money matters to a partner: it pays to keep your eye on the ball in this area of traditional male prerogative. And don't worry, because it's not always as complicated as they like to make out.

Although the issues around money may appear to be overwhelming from time to time, allow yourself to trust that life will bring you what you need. It usually does. None the less, there are sensible, down-to-earth measures we can take in order to protect ourselves and lead a relatively secure existence. It helps to remember that older people are big players in the economy: the retired in the UK alone spend £25 billion annually (84 per cent buy holidays, 72 per cent buy cars and 43 per cent buy financial services). Seventy per cent of European investors trading in stocks and shares over the Internet are over 50. This is power. We can afford to be confident and assertive in our dealings with people over money, not victims setting ourselves up to be ripped off.

Organising your finances

- Get a decent filing cabinet if you haven't already got one. Mark the drawers clearly.
- If you are changing your work pattern, or retiring, work out your sources of income. For example:
    - state pension and benefits
    - private pensions (from work or from personal schemes)
    - interest from any savings and investments
    - any pay you are likely to get from your new work
    - any maturing insurance policies
    - any inheritances
- Seek financial advice if you feel you need it, but don't assume that you won't be ripped off. Try the Internet first; there are numerous excellent sites offering advice for free, and you can take your pick (see Resources, page 204). I stick to this actually – it's fairly common advice on radio programmes that specialize in money matters, and my personal experience with financial advisers has not impressed me.
- Magazines aimed at executive retirement, and weekend papers, often have useful information and advice.
- Work out how much you need to spend on the

basics of life, bearing in mind that certain expenses may fluctuate (See Detailed budget planner, page 175).
- Decide whether you need to accumulate income, to increase your savings, to convert your assets, to invest at high or low risk, or to learn about market conditions in order to create a model portfolio for yourself. For this, you need to set goals.

Setting Goals

In order to clarify your priorities, ask yourself the following questions:

- What is more important to you in your life: quality or quantity?
- Are you set on staying where you live, or would you consider smaller accommodation?
- Do you need your car or are you happy to make savings (and be ecologically friendly too) by using public transport and taxis? How

important is it to you to be mobile in terms of travelling around, bearing in mind the possible isolation of growing older?

- Which interests do you now want (and can you afford) to pursue that you had no time for in a full-time working life? What will they cost you?
- Do you want to leave an inheritance, or to spend all your money while you can enjoy it?
- Explore the 'devil in the detail' by working out from last year's invoices your current costs in

food and household, utilities, medical care, clothing, vacations, children, savings etc. Set this against your sources of income (see above) and make a realistic target for living comfortably and happily within the margin of these two.

Planning For and In Retirement

Here are some basic questions you should ask yourself:

- What will be my retirement income? My retirement outgoings?
- What changes should I make in my financial planning?
- What will my living expenses be when I retire?
- What social security benefits will I have?
- What will my pension be?
- Will there be interest off investments?
- What will my tax position be?
- Should I move into a smaller place?
- Should I raise capital on my home?
- Should I adapt my home in a different way to suit my new needs? Take a lodger for example?

Detailed budget planner

Even if you hate doing it, you can't ignore the fact that you have to organise – at least to some degree – your budget. Once it's organised, you can relax. My top tip is to be on good terms with your accountant, so that phoning him/her is a pleasure not a chore. The relationship factor is paramount.

It may be useful to make a list from the following suggestions, adding anything extra that applies especially to you. Make a balance sheet for yourself including the following headings, and work out your tax position.

Basic outgoings

Food, rent or mortgage, council tax, repair and maintenance, heating, lighting, phone, TV licence or rental, household insurance, clothes, laundry and cleaners, car and other transport, regular savings, loan repayments, healthcare.

Extra expenditure

Holidays, presents, books and newspapers, drink and cigarettes, hair and beauty products, entertainment, subscriptions, covenants, pets, etc.

When making your calculations, don't forget inflation and build this in at about 4 per cent per annum. And make a will: dying intestate presents painful complications to your nearest relatives which are costly in solicitors' fees, and your estate may not end up where you would have wished. If you die intestate your estate goes to your closest living relative. There are ways of making your own will (see Resources, page 204), but if you want help, consult a solicitor.

Possible savings you can make

These may include reducing: insurance contributions, pension contributions, cost of travel to work, lunches, drinks with colleagues, work clothes. You could stop smoking. In addition you may qualify for free medical prescriptions, free eye tests, concessionary travel, mature driver's insurance and life assurance premiums. If you move to a small house your bills could become smaller, and your children may become less dependent, and you may be in a lower tax bracket. Cutbacks don't have to be negative: the most important ingredient of your lifestyle is your relationships and friendships, not the colour of your bank balance.

Saving money on utilities

If you are changing to working from home, or retiring from work so that you spend more time at home, it's well worth looking at the savings you can make on your energy bills.

- Insulate your roof.
- Well-lined curtains keep the heat in better than thin ones.
- Use energy-saving light bulbs.
- Use draught-excluders along the bottom of doors.
- Insulate your hot water tank.
- Consider switching your supplier: some companies offer discounts, or at least better value for money.

Possible extra outgoings

If you are now spending more time at home your heating and lighting bills may increase, your leisure activities cost more, you may have to replace your company car, you may need to take out private health insurance, and possibly have out-of-pocket expenses for voluntary work. You may want to pay people to do practical jobs around the house and garden which become harder to do, or which you wish to delegate, and to increase the level of your home comforts.

Possible sources of income

Before tax:
Pensions: state, personal or employment; other state benefits, casual work or other pre-tax earnings. You may decide to raise income off property, by renting or in schemes whereby you can take out a loan against the value of your property when you die, or a home reversion plan whereby you sell all or part of your home in return or a lifetime income and lifetime tenancy.

After tax:
Dividends from investments, bank deposit accounts, building society interest, annuity income, and any other tax-free receipts such as investment bond withdrawals, national savings interest etc.

Pensions

If you are still working it is worth considering whether to contribute more to your pension fund. It is a tax-efficient way of saving. But do scan the small print carefully: there are numerous pension schemes where contributors fail to realise that the capital sum reverts to the company on death of the contributor. This may not be part of your plan:

you may wish your capital to go elsewhere. So study the agreement carefully, or seek professional advice. You may decide that investing your capital in bonds or building societies will give you a safer and better return on your money.

If you have a state pension, make sure that you meet the necessary contributions qualifications, and that you claim it a few months prior to reaching the age due to receive it.

Your retirement benefits will be based on the value of the contributions and bonuses that have built up over the years. Some personal pension plans offer a flexible retirement age, from 50 upwards, but if you claim a pension before the age specified you will almost always be penalised. Some people opt to invest in annuities, which are indexed against future inflation. It is best to take advice from an expert on this, since opinion is divided between those who regard annuities as decidedly dodgy, and those who can talk you into their virtues.

Social security

Depending on which country you live in, you may qualify for social security benefits of which you are unaware. The best advice is to get on to the Internet and get your national information from the numerous websites on financial affairs (see Resources, page 204). In general, though, you may be able to claim income support, housing benefit, council tax or rates reductions, jobseeker's allowance, attendance allowance for caring for an elderly relative, invalid care allowance, disability living allowance, and to get lump sums from a social fund to help with such things as funerals or heating during severe weather. You may qualify for help with healthcare, with house repairs or for help with residential or nursing home fees. Concessions may be available on TV licences and travel, and if widowed you may be paid various widows' benefits.

Insurances

The good news about getting older is that certain types of insurance offer discounts on premiums as well as no-claims. Motor insurance is one area where age is an advantage, so check with your company that you are not paying over the odds once you pass a certain birthday. Travel is another area where excellent rates can be found through specialist companies. If you have lived in your home for a long time, do make sure that your valuation is up to date, since an increase in property prices will affect your position if you have to claim. Bear in mind too that when replacing possessions you will have to pay today's rates and not those of yesteryear when you first acquired them, which could mean that you're seriously underinsured. Researching it thoroughly and having the right information gives you power and makes it less likely that you will be ripped off.

Health insurance is, increasingly, a huge issue. If you decide to take out a private healthcare option, do it earlier rather than later, when you are in good health, otherwise your premium may be more than you want to pay in relation to your income. Thinking ahead on this one could really pay off. Seek impartial advice before committing yourself to a particular company.

You may wish to insure yourself to cover any debts you may have and to provide for your dependants, in which case it is worth considering an endowment policy where you pay regular premiums over a 10–25-year period in return for a tax-free lump sum on a specified date. If you die before that date, the remaining payments are waived and the lump sum reverts to your dependants. Withdrawing early from such schemes however can involve heavy penalties, so make sure that this sort of long-term commitment is one you can easily afford.

Tax

Your tax position may well alter if you change employment, start a new business, go freelance, or stop working altogether. Pick up information at your local tax office, your accountant or ask a financial adviser to help guide you through this change. You will need to tell them about:

- any income you're still earning
- tax-free income from maturing investments
- any rents you gain through letting rooms
- details of any redundancy payment
- gifts
- social security payments
- allowances

- tax-free sums earned from personal or occupational pensions

You can then establish what, if any, tax allowances you are entitled to, and subtract them from your income, incorporating the personal tax-free allowance, and other allowances if appropriate. The sum that is left is what you are taxed on. There may be tax relief due to you also, for example a widow's bereavement allowance, a married couple's allowance etc.

This is a very rough guide to get you started. It is important to study the finer details, in order to make sure you get all your dues. It may also be in your interest to study the capital gains tax and its exemptions, and to look for ways of minimising inheritance tax by making early bequests, gifts and donations. Setting up a trust for your descendants is an option for those in the upper income groups.

Savings and investments

Advice on savings can be sought over the Internet (see Resources, page 204) or from financial advisers, actuaries, accountants, bank managers, insurance salespersons, solicitors and stockbrokers. Some advisers can offer help only within their own organisations, whereas an independent financial adviser should be able to give you a wider picture. There are excellent magazines and financial papers (see Resources, page 204), as well as some radio programmes that offer helpful guidance.

You need to be clear in your own mind whether you want to aim for capital growth (i.e. increase the lump sum of your savings), or income from the interest off that capital. Consider whether you are prepared to take risks with your money, and bear in mind any future financial commitments or plans.

Low risk

National savings certificates and bonds
Building society accounts
Bank deposit accounts
Gilts
Guaranteed income bonds
Premium bonds

Medium risk

Unit trusts, equity plans
Investment trusts with well-spread funds
Single premium unit-linked bonds

High risk

Playing the stock market (This is a gamble: you may make a fortune or lose your money. You need to know what you are doing, or be very lucky. You could try dummy runs by choosing shares as if you were going to invest in them, then watching their progress. This way you can learn about companies and pick up both information and confidence if you do decide to have a portfolio of shares.)
Shares
Specialist funds
Specific companies

play it
safe

play it safe

Personal security can often seem to become more of an issue the older we get, and many of us worry about it. However, a great deal of it is in the mind: if we think confidently, we run less risk of attack, whereas if we give out signs of fear we appear more vulnerable. It is well known that bullies pick on victims who give themselves away by their body language – particular ways of walking or looking or holding the head down that signal fear. The more self-confident we both are and appear to be, and the less anxious, the less likely we are to be attacked. One of the most valuable assets that we can cultivate for this time in our lives, therefore, is the mental and physical language of assurance. Learning to breathe deeply and calmly (see the exercises on page 136) as we walk alone has a powerful effect on quietening fear, making it less likely that we will be mugged.

That being said, you must be streetwise of course, take sensible precautions, and be alert to danger. Walking through a city at night, it is as well to have a screech alarm in your hand. It is not a good idea to park in underground car parks alone at night. Dark unlit back streets can be dangerous places. Generally speaking you are safer in a twosome than walking alone. Keep your driving licence for as long as you can – it gives you an important sense of independence.

It is useful to keep a sense of perspective: the highest rate of victimisation in violent crime occurs in the 16-24 age group, the lowest in the 65-74 age group. Police figures show that you are 18 times less likely to be attacked if you are over 60 than someone aged 16-29. So don't allow your fear of attack to stop you going out and to render you housebound (where you are just as likely to die from loneliness and depression)!

Tips for personal safety

- Carry a screech alarm (see page 187) in your hand when walking through towns or cities alone, especially at night.
- Carry a mobile phone with you, but keep it out of the sight of thieves.
- Don't carry large amounts of cash around with you.
- Wear a belt-bag under your coat rather than carrying a handbag.
- Avoid walking through badly lit streets, wasteland, commons or alleyways.
- Avoid parking in multi-storey car parks when you are alone.
- Park in a well-lit spot.

- Always close windows and sun-roofs, even if you are only leaving the car for a little while.
- Don't wear or carry valuables or objects of sentimental value – leave them at home in a safe place.
- Have your keys ready in your hand as you approach your house so that you can get inside quickly.
- Carry your house keys in your coat pocket in case your bag is snatched.
- Wear your wallet in an inside pocket or body-purse.
- While you are waiting for a train or a bus, stand with your back to a wall so that nobody can surprise you from behind.
- Walk facing the traffic so that a car cannot pull up behind you.
- Be alert to the need for extra caution as you pass side entrances to garages or alleyways.
- Don't display valuable items of shopping inside the car – lock them in the boot.
- If someone tries to snatch your bag it may be wiser not to struggle; the injury you risk may not be worth it.
- Take a course in self-defence – sooner rather than later while you are fit and *before* the event of an attack: it's fun, and well worth it for the peace of mind that it gives you. Some courses teach 'streetwise' tips too.
- Most burglaries take place during the day when you are out at work. Getting to know your neighbours, quite apart from the friendship value, means that you can look out for one another and keep an eye on each other's houses. Neighbourhood Watch works in liaison with the police and you can set up a group in collaboration with them.

Protecting your home

Surprisingly, statistics show that older people are *less* likely to be burgled than the young: 3.5 per cent of households where the householder is aged 65-74 as opposed to 15.2 per cent where they are between 16 and 24. Nevertheless there are reasonable precautions that are worth taking, just as much from a practical security angle as for your own peace of mind. A crime-prevention officer will give you a free security survey of your house and offer impartial advice. And make sure that you are as well insured as you would wish to be (see page 177) so that, if necessary, you will at least be compensated to some degree for the losses incurred.

Not far off in the future the 'smart home' awaits. With an integrated computer system we will be able to activate by remote control door and window locks, curtains and blinds, heating, lighting and security devices, video surveillance and much else. This degree of contact with our homes will give us greater security from a distance and render obsolete many of the current practices we use to protect ourselves and our property. But here, for now, are some practical tips to provide you with at least a degree of peace of mind on how to protect your home.

Making Your Front Door Secure

- Make sure that your door is sturdy and made of solid wood or PVC, at least 44mm (1³/₄in) thick, with a strong frame. Glass-panelled doors are obviously more vulnerable.
- Have your door fitted with a spy-hole or viewer, a wide-angle lens that enables you to see your caller. Fit a strong security chain. This means that you can check your caller's credentials without admitting him or her to your house.
- Fit a mortice lock with at least 5 levers (BS3621), sometimes called a 'Chubb' lock. A second 'Yale' lock may be opened not only by key but by a lever on the inside.

- Try the following process to put off bogus callers (who may look perfectly respectable and authentic) claiming to be service officials: ask to see their ID, and if you are in doubt, close the door on them and ring the company to check. If you are still concerned, ring the police. Don't allow salespersons into your home: keep them on the doorstep.
- 'Workman fraud', where people do repairs to the exterior of your house, uninvited, and then demand payment, is a hazard to be on the lookout for. Be prepared to call the police.
- An entryphone is a useful checking device.
- You may wish to install mortice security bolts for extra protection: they are stronger than old-fashioned bolts and should be fitted about 22.5cm (9in) from the top and bottom of the door. Hinge bolts protect the hinge side of the door from being forced.

Look at Your House From a Burglar's Point of View

- Some people don't bother much about security at the back of their property, but at least 64 per cent of burglars enter through the rear. It's advisable to put similar locks on to back and side doors as on the front door (see left).
- Windows are just as vulnerable entry points as doors, even small ones, especially if they are on the ground floor, particularly at the rear of the house, and near a flat roof. Fasten them with security locks and keep them locked unless you use the room regularly. Keep the keys nearby for convenience, but well out of sight of burglars.
- Don't leave keys in locks even when you have locked up, and especially if your doors have glass panelling.
- Exterior lighting at the front and back of your house is a useful device to deter thieves. You can install lighting that is triggered by infrared sensors, which indicates that someone is approaching the house. It also helps you to find your keys and unlock your door in the dark!
- General police advice is to lock your outer doors even if you are just watching TV: 27 per cent of burglars in 1990 simply walked into their victim's houses.
- Even if you are just 'popping out' to the shops or to a neighbour, do not leave doors and windows unlocked. Sometimes you will be out for longer than you intended, and a burglar may be watching your house. It takes only a matter of minutes for someone to enter and exit with your valuables.
- Draw your curtains if you go out for the evening so that a burglar can't see in.
- Never leave spare keys under a doormat or flowerpot or dustbin. It'll be the first place an intruder is likely to look.
- Don't leave spare keys in an obvious place indoors when you go out, otherwise a burglar, having forced entry through a window, can easily unlock the door and walk out with your possessions.
- Cancel deliveries when you go away. The classic

telltale sign to a would-be thief is a pile of papers on the doormat that is visible through a window. Ask your post office to keep your mail until you return (give them a week's notice).

- Use time switches to make lights go on and off to make it look as if someone is at home.
- Leave a radio on, even when you go out for a short while, so that it sounds as if someone is at home.

Useful Tips

- If you have a friendly neighbour whom you can trust, give them a set of spare keys so that you are not in dire straits if you lock yourself out, lose your own keys, or even need help when you are indoors. You can do the same for them. These informal relationships become more, not less, important as we grow older.
- If you are burgled, or lose your keys, change your locks immediately.
- Keep the name and number of a good locksmith handy.
- Don't attach your name and address to your bunch of keys – this is an open invitation.
- Put a 'Beware dangerous dogs' notice on your gate, and keep a mailbox outside the gate. It works wonders at deterring unwanted callers of all kinds.
- It's worth marking your more precious belongings with your postcode, using a special indelible kit available from DIY stores, some stationers, or crime prevention officers.

- If you have antiques, silver, precious heirlooms or jewellery, photograph them and lock the photos away so that if they are stolen the police can help identify them if found.
- Note down the serial numbers of your TV, VCR, camera, radios, microwave etc. to help identify your property if stolen.
- Keep a checklist in your diary of credit card, building society, bank account, cashpoint card numbers etc., and the relevant emergency telephone numbers, so that in the event of theft you can advise them immediately.
- Don't keep large amounts of cash at home.
- Keep valuable jewellery in a safe or in the bank, not under the bed.
- Keep your garden sheds locked.
- Keep your bicycle locked up.

Alarm Systems

Intruder alarms

Burglar alarms that are visible from the outside make a burglar think twice. Have a bell alarm installed that you activate when you go out and which goes off if an intruder enters. You can choose from a remote control-operated device, or a panel on to which you punch a code, or a key-operated control. You may choose to install a system that is connected to your local police station, a service for which there is usually a fee. Alarm systems that sound like huge dogs barking loudly are also available. They are triggered by the intruder and just the noise is enough to send them packing. Never allow a travelling salesman to do this installation; make sure you get someone from a reputable and reliable company.

Personal attack alarms

A small device with a panic button that you can hold in your hand while walking alone is one of the most reassuring methods of personal security. You can obtain 'screech alarms' through police stations, some chain stores and DIY centres.

Social alarms

An emergency response alarm that you wear around your neck or clipped to your clothing allows you to call for help in case of accident or emergency from anywhere in the house. It sends a radio signal to a unit plugged into a telephone socket and automatically dials a programmed number to an emergency operator.

Fire Security

- Smoke alarms: apparently people over 60 run the lowest risk of having a fire at home, but nevertheless a smoke alarm is simple to install and is an early warning of an incipient fire, giving you time to call the emergency services. Put it in a hallway or upstairs landing – not too close to your kitchen otherwise it will go off all the time! It could make the difference between life and death.
- Keep a fire-blanket next to your oven and hob.
- Never throw water on to burning oil or fat fires – it causes the fire to spread (oil floats on water).
- Make sure that you have secure fireguards for electric or gas heaters, as well as for an open wood or coal fire.
- Never leave clothes drying in front of a fire.
- Never move a heater while it is switched on.
- If people smoke in your house, make sure that there are decent-size ashtrays around, and always make sure that no cigarette is left smouldering but that it is stubbed out.
- Never smoke in bed. Many fire accidents, including fatalities, happen this way.
- Keep fire extinguishers at focal points in the house to deal with small fires.
- Call emergency help immediately in the event of a fire that you have no hope of dealing with. Fire gets out of control extremely fast.
- Check the instructions on your electric blanket carefully and follow them, and never use one that shows signs of wear and tear.

Victim Support

If you are unfortunate enough to become the victim of a crime, try not to let it overwhelm you and poison your life. Share your feelings with a good friend, and think as positively as you can. Support schemes are offered for victims of crime (see Resources, page 204) through which counsellors will visit you in your home and offer practical and emotional support. The police will put you in touch with your local scheme on request.

enjoy
yourself

enjoy yourself

Too much of a good thing is wonderful Mae West

Go for it

Now is the time to enjoy yourself. Not later. Don't postpone your fun: after all, how much longer have you got? Now is the time to shed the pointless guilt around having a good time doing what you want to do and to explore one of the most important areas on the map of your life. You may not get another chance.

Enjoyment entails balance. A life spent in hedonistic self-pampering is more likely to end in boredom than in paradise. Balance is a surface tension between interfacing parts of life (pleasure and work, exercise and rest, good food and simplicity in living), so in spite of Mae West's witty aphorism you *can* have too much of a good thing! But adjusting from years of hard work and relative self-sacrifice to integrating less work with more pleasure and leisure and self-fulfilment in your life, can provide a healthy and creative balance. Those around you will benefit as much as you do. This is the time of your life to move

beyond (yet not necessarily out of) the defining identity of work.

The guilt trap is hard to shake off. But guilt can become an excuse for not doing things. By definition, guilt is self-centred, its object a deflection from which are projected blame and judgement. It is negative energy. Guilt is a form of self-indulgence, and it can become a diverting justification, offering an escape route from constructive action and from taking responsibility. When my friend Anna walked out of her job after a flaming row with her boss, she realised that she had let her closest and long-term colleague down very badly. Rather than facing up to her and saying how sorry she genuinely was, she refused to see her again and carried the guilt around with her instead. In place of the freedom she had longed for, she was imprisoned by her own feelings.

Guilt is culturally determined by social regulation and religious dogma. The straitjacket of

our conditioning fits all too well if we submit to it. Being all things to all men, being 'perfect' (please!), being successful (by whose criteria?) are parts of an ideological construct that has an unseen but tight grip on our lives. Shaking that loose can be one of the greatest liberations of maturity. This is summed up neatly in the words of Katharine Hepburn: 'If you obey all the rules you miss all the fun.'

A happy balance of work and leisure, of physical and mental stimulation, of duty and pleasure, of creativity and indolence, breeds contentment and fulfilment. This is the age at which to expand a portfolio of interests, of friendships and other relationships, and of learning. It is the age to do the things you love to do, to make your own way, not feeling confined to the dictates of what others are doing, but rather to invent a new world for yourself, and to take risks. It is the age at which to let go of the internal censor, that tireless critic that goes 'you ought to be doing this' or 'you shouldn't do that' (because it is giving you too much pleasure, or because nobody else is doing it). True maturity means widening horizons. It does *not* have to mean the stereotypical expansion of the waistline and narrowing of the mind: instead of meekly accepting this life-sentence, why not turn it on its head and make the opposite true? You can be the one to turn that around. The self-knowledge, self-definition and self-assurance that come through fulfilling our heretofore-unrealised dreams, is what true maturity means. Anaïs Nin wrote that 'life is

a process of becoming, a combination of states we have to go through. Where people fail is that they wish to elect a state and remain in it.'

Research at Hull University and elsewhere has demonstrated that the sheer enjoyment derived from simple pleasures more than outweighs the damage done to our health if we feel guilty about them. Guilt comes with a health warning. It is a major stressor. Many illnesses are caused by stress. People who feel the most guilty when indulging in their favourite activities have weaker defences against infection. Yes, guilt affects your immune system. Those people with the highest pleasure/guilt ratio in their lives (more pleasure than guilt) have high levels of immunoglobulin, and therefore more effective immune systems. More of these people, it so happens, are male than female. Guilt is a predominantly female disorder. You have been warned!

Perhaps we take ourselves too seriously. Ethel Barrymore said, 'You grow up the day you have your first real laugh – at yourself.' Laughter is one of the pathways to good health both mental and physical and if you don't laugh at yourself you'll miss a lot of the jokes. The British nation's favourite poem of 1995 (see right) describes the relief of sending oneself up in the process of becoming who one wants to be.

The Art of Self-altruism

'Well-behaved women rarely make history,' said Laurel Thatcher Ulrich. You don't have to be 'good' any more, 'to behave'. You can be joyous, you can have a ball. Keeping your sense of humour in good repair, being able to laugh at yourself as well as at life, lubricates this process of allowing yourself to be happy. Of *learning* to be happy even. Because that is not a serious element of our conditioning (apart from the fairytale of perfect love which was inherently doomed to failure.) The iron rod of guilt was there whether acknowledged or not. Now you can pick it up and throw it away. You may (to mix the metaphor) be overwhelmed by the feeling of relief at no longer having to run after a moving bus.

Learning happiness may involve taking risks, and taking risks may mean making mistakes ('to err is human – but it feels divine' is the divine Mae West's riposte to that). Now is the time to surrender to the temptation (Mae West again: 'I generally avoid temptation unless I can't resist it'), to sort out your life, to start new ventures, to allow parts of your personality full rein. Take this opportunity to draw up a new map for your life free of the stuff that is past its sell-by date, to create new pathways, new attitudes, new adventures, new relationships and new routines. Go for it. Whether you want to trek in the Himalayas, or run a soup kitchen, learn to fly, take a degree, or write a book (Mary Wesley wrote her first bestseller at 70), move house, take a lover, travel around the world or learn to dance – now is the time. 'If you always do what interests you,' said Katharine Hepburn wisely, 'then at least one person is pleased.'

Warning

When I am an old woman I shall wear purple
With a red hat which doesn't go, and doesn't suit me,
And I shall spend my pension on brandy and summer
    gloves
And satin sandals, and say we've no money for butter.
I shall sit down on the pavement when I'm tired
And gobble up samples in shops and press alarm bells
And run my stick along the public railings
And make up for the sobriety of my youth.
I shall go out in my slippers in the rain
And pick the flowers in other people's gardens
And learn to spit.

You can wear terrible shirts and grow more fat
And eat three pounds of sausages at a go
Or only bread and pickle for a week
And hoard pens and pencils and beermats and things in
    boxes.

But now we must have clothes that keep us dry
And pay our rent and not swear in the street
And set a good example for the children.
We must have friends for dinners and read the papers.

But maybe I ought to practise a little now?
So people who know me are not too shocked and
    surprised
When suddenly I am old, and start to wear purple.

Jenny Joseph

Not Enough Time to Enjoy Yourself

The author and barrister John Mortimer said that as you get older it seems that it's always breakfast time again. *Tempus fugit* as my classicist father used to say. Personally I find that the older I get the more things there are that interest me and the fewer hours in the day to indulge them. Today's information overload doesn't help. Paradoxically the only way to slow down this alarming increase of speed in the passage of time is to slow down oneself – and then you get more fitted in. It works. Even a short meditation at the beginning of the day opens up that mental and physical space (see page 71). Try the following too.

- Get up earlier (and enjoy the quiet part of the day!).
- Do one thing at a time, with total focus.
- Make 'to-do' lists.
- Plan. Big things (year planners), small things (household chores) and long-term projects (that book you are going to write...).
- Allow other people to do things for you. It's called the Art of Delegation.
- Daydream. It's good for your health, as well as for your imagination (and sometimes dreams do come true).
- Learn to breathe (see page 136) and meditate (see page 71).
- Take time out to read.
- Pamper yourself (massages, facials etc. – see pages 96-113).
- Listen to your favourite music.
- Go on retreat: it creates amazing head-space.

Retreats are available in many forms, not all of them religion-based (see Resources, page 204).

- Laugh a lot.
- Do what you want to do, and not what you don't.
- Start having fun.
- Remember that life is in the here and now and not in the there and afterwards.

If you follow these guidelines, you won't have any time to be ill. You will keep yourself young at heart. This is good for society at large since it means that you will not be a drain on its medical health resources. The young will be grateful for this: they will not be forced to bear the extra financial burden, let alone worry about us. The composer Nadia Boulanger said, 'The essential conditions of everything you do must be choice, love, passion.' Following this guiding passion will give you the time of your life, the time that you deserve, it will turn every day into a celebration. Body Shop's Anita Roddick has spoken of how passion has been the greatest driving force of her life, and the outcome of that energy is awe-inspiring. If your life does not have this passion, make a fresh start. Get out there and find it, mix with people who have it, and wake up your mind. Mental agility is the key (see Brain Power, page 56), and it is never too late. Nothing is impossible. This message has not been lost on women over 50 in the West: they are a powerful force not merely in the consumer market where they dominate the leisure and travel industries, but a potent force for change, for moving forward into the 21st century.

Creativity

Taking up a creative activity can open up new horizons in your life. It can help relieve stress by absorbing you so that you forget your problems for while, and gain a clearer perspective on them.

Everyone is creative. Everyone has creative potential, and mid-life is a great time to explore that energy whether or not you have used it before in your life. Creativity is a bit like a muscle: it needs exercising in order to improve it and bring it to 'fitness'. The training may at first be arduous, and sometimes disheartening, but perseverance pays off. You may feel shy, inadequate, uncomfortable, but it's profitable to learn to see these feelings as part of the learning curve that you are on. I started horse-riding at the age of 50 and it was excruciating: physically uncomfortable (how my seat hurt to start with), psychologically humiliating (being taught by teenagers was bad enough, but I was also inept), emotionally draining (I was terrified). A lot of the time I spent wishing I was at home curled up on the sofa with a book, but eventually it turned into one of the greatest pleasures of my life. There was a huge lesson there for me about not needing to be 'perfect'. I didn't have to become an Olympic dressage champion, I could happily opt for hacking quietly around the countryside through the four seasons, without worrying about whether I was 'good' at it or not. I was 'good enough' and that was sufficient.

'Find the passion,' said Agnes de Mille. 'It takes great passion and great energy to do anything creative. I would go so far as to say that you can't do it without that passion.' Allow yourself to rediscover it (it's there!) and to uncover your innate creativity: Picasso said that every child is an artist but the problem is staying an artist when you grow up; so we have to become children again, as it were, exploring, finding delight in, becoming absorbed, connecting with the magic and fun in life, learning to *play*.

If you don't believe you are a creative person (and there is nobody who is not) there are always ways of accessing your hidden talents. One key to unlocking creativity of any kind is to write three pages longhand each morning when you wake up. Just write. It doesn't matter what: just dump the flotsam and jetsam floating at the top of your mind, the rubbish, the great thoughts, the feelings. Even writing 'I don't know what to say...' is fine. These 'morning pages' are never to be read, by you or by anyone; they are not literature, they are free associations just tumbled out on to the page leaving a space for clarity and creativity to arise. The demented monkey-mind is given free expression and then, satisfied, will give you a bit of peace. These 'morning pages' are the mental equivalent of blowing your nose. The offloading clears the way for something deeper to breathe from under the smothering surface of the twittering mind.

Like the body, our creative nature needs to stretch and exercise otherwise it gets blocked. Unblocking the pathways of this energy is the job of these jottings, this expression of the trivial detail of life as we map our interior lives. In doing so we get *ourselves* out of the way in order for 'it' to flow: we pull focus, we become less self-involved and more aware of life around us in what is, paradoxically, the antithesis of self-consciousness. This process of writing 'morning pages' works not just for writers, but for dancers, actors, lawyers, sculptors, sportsmen, housewives, grandmothers, students and people of all kinds and ages. For everyone. It is never too late to start. Creativity is as intrinsic to your nature as your blood is to the body and the refusal to be creative is like the behaviour of a stubborn child whose wilfulness goes against the tide of his nature.

The creative recovery that comes through this process is a bumpy journey. You go through irritation, boredom, despair and much negativity and then suddenly you see what is happening. Just by rattling on over the pages you begin to recognise your internal censor, and as you go on you start to care less what it says, that critical voice inside your head hissing like a snake in the grass that you are no good and what's the point. You begin to learn how to deal with this constant uninvited critic. You become more observant, you start to both see and hear things with more definition, and it is this detail that counts and that is so effective. Images, feelings, sounds, sights and tastes constitute that sensory magic which is the electricity of artistic communication. You realise that you don't have to be Chekhov or Rembrandt: that just getting the detail down is magic in itself and the bigger picture will take care of itself. You

may find you want and need to have a notebook
and pencil with you as you move around in your
everyday life, for jotting down impressions and
ideas as they occur to you. I carry a micro-tape-
recorder with me in the car and on long walks, so
that I can record anything that occurs to me
spontaneously and freely, without artifice. It's
amazing what you get when you transcribe it.
Look, observe, eavesdrop, and you will find
yourself enjoying a richer tapestry of life than you
ever experienced before.

Add to this at least two hours a week of some
creative activity in which you can lose yourself,
some treat to yourself that does not involve
anyone else. Watch a movie, go to an exhibition
or museum, go for a long walk in the countryside,
arrange some flowers, take yourself off to the
theatre, listen to music, walk along the beach, go
riding, nose around a junk-shop, have a long soak
in an aromatic bath, play the piano, do some
cooking, or do something really lowbrow for a
change like going to a funfair or a theme park or
watching a TV soap. Taking time out for this self-
nourishing, in whatever form it takes, fertilises the
ground for your creativity to grow. Creative activity
is good for the soul. It is also a kind of self-
definition. Don't postpone: do it now! Start to play!

Areas to explore
Here are some suggestions for possible options:
- films, film-making, video production, film studies
- music-making: choirs, singing lessons, playing

instruments, hand-bells
- exploring museums
- nature, wildlife, conservation, ecology
- bee-keeping
- creative writing courses, poetry
- starting a reading circle for play-readings, poetry or literary fiction
- the world of the theatre and drama
- visual arts: contemporary and national art collections
- crafts: textiles, embroidery, furniture, ceramics etc.
- painting and sculpture and the decorative arts
- dance: folk dancing, salsa, jazz, ballet, contemporary dance
- history, archaeology, architecture
- astronomy, meteorology, cosmology, geology
- gardens, gardening, garden design
- genealogy
- women's groups where you can share common interests and experiences with a degree of social freedom
- photography
- flying, paragliding, gliding
- horses, dogs, working with animals

Travel

The travel industry has flourished recently from the new footloose spirit of the over-50s. You can opt for simple breaks-for-pleasure, or holidays that give you a mixture of physical and mental activity, or adventure, strenuous exercise, or a completely new experience to keep your mind lively and open. Tourism may or may not appeal to you, and if it does there is no shortage of brochures to tempt you to the farthest flung corners of the globe, from around-the-world cruises to exploring the Far East to Great Train Journeys of the World. If this type of tourism is not for you, there are special interest holidays organised with the over-50s age group in mind, there are study holidays, and you can always go on retreat. Retreat centres provide a wonderful opportunity to 'stop', to detach, to experience deep peace and refreshment which have a long-lasting effect when one returns to everyday living (see Resources, page 204).

One of the problems with mainstream organised travel is the cost of the single-room supplement. However, some travel firms offer supplement-free holidays (see Resources, page 204), and it is worth hunting these out in order to avoid the sometimes substantial added cost, where you can comfortably travel within the company of a loosely organised group and have your own private room. If you are anxious about travelling on your own, there are also organisations for putting travel-companions in touch with each other. (See Resources, page 204.)

If you live in the Northern Hemisphere and hate the long grey winters, you could choose some of the long winter breaks offered by some travel companies that are often incredibly good value. You might consider a house-sitter for the time you are away, or to let out your home property on a short tenancy.

Special Interest Breaks

For those people who prefer active holidays, there is a wide range to choose from in the realms of special interest breaks and study holidays. They range through archaeology, gardens, golf, painting, walking, visiting the battlefields of the two world wars, sports of all kinds including watersports like scuba diving and deep-sea diving. Some specific models include:

- music festivals – Bayreuth (Wagner), Salzburg (Mozart), Eisenstadt (Haydn), Vienna, Verona and other festivals held at the great opera houses of Europe and the USA
- *The Passion Play* at Oberammergau in Austria
- pilgrimages to Mecca or Jerusalem, Santiago de Compostela in Spain, Assisi in Italy, the Holy Land, great cathedrals of England or France etc.
- horse-riding holidays all over the world from Argentina and Patagonia to Mongolia, Montana or Wyoming, India, Jordan, Africa, Italy, Spain and Portugal
- botanical expeditions such as those run by top lecturers from Kew Gardens in London
- cycling holidays in Provence or Tuscany
  And many more ...

Study Holidays

Many university extra-curricular departments run study breaks, from single days to weekends to week-long courses. They also organise summer schools. Cambridge University, through their centre at Madingley Hall, offers studies in the ancient world and archaeology, art, architecture and the decorative arts, history, local and landscape history, language, literature, music, natural sciences, philosophy, psychology, religion, society and civilisation, and film studies.

Study tours are also offered by many organisations including the Association for Cultural Exchange (see Resources, page 204). Experienced lecturers take groups all over the world to study musicians and composers, painters, architecture, art, history, history of art, garden history and gardens, birds, flowers, fauna, palaces and temples, and much more.

With such a lot on offer, how can we fail to enjoy ourselves? Let's leave the wage-slaves to it and spread our wings. I'm off to Sri Lanka to look at Buddhist temples and bird sanctuaries.

A final thought...

In Lakota native American culture there are three stages of life: from 0-11 you are a 'sacred being', from 12-45 a 'youth'. For the rest of your life you are a 'real person'.

resources

The new woman

Recommended reading

Debate Of The Age – The Millennium Papers

Pamphlets available through Age Concern (see below)

The issues addressed include employment and how it gives structure and meaning to life, in terms of self-esteem and the importance of a place in the community. Involvement in the community, education and training, retirement lifestyles, social care and welfare, housing, future design and technology, transport, local services and facilities, the regeneration of deprived areas, ironing out inequalities in healthcare, finance, pensions and welfare reforms and how society will pay for its ageing population including disability benefits, and support for carers. These fundamental areas affect us all regardless of age, whatever country we live in, and give a panoramic view of the scope and dimension of the challenges ahead.

Freedom!

Recommended reading

J. Beck, *Cognitive Therapy: Basics and Beyond* (NY Guildford, 1995)

Contacts

For information on cognitive therapy:

www.mindstreet.com

www.figurehead.clara.net

Choices, choices

Recommended reading

Rosemary Brown, *The Good Non-retirement Guide* (updated yearly), Kogan Page, *The Which Guide to Active Retirement* (updated yearly), Consumer's Association, *The Voluntary Agencies Directory*, NCVO (updated yearly)

Contacts

UK Resources

TECS (Local Trading and Enterprise Councils)

0800 100 900

Provide support in setting up a new business.

LETS (Local Exchange and Trading Schemes)

Contact details from local community centre.

A 'barter'-based alternative to paid work.

Age Concern

020 8679 8000

www.ageconcern.org.uk

Runs workshops for identifying skills under 'Age Resource'. Useful practical information on their Factsheet 31 'Older Workers'.

Employers' Forum on Age

020 8765 7280

Information for employers.

REACH

020 7928 0452

Part-time expenses-only jobs for professionals.

RSVP (Retired Senior Voluntary Programmes)

020 7278 6601

For voluntary work.

Business in the Community

020 7224 1600

Offers a wide range of advice.

BBC
08700 100 222
www.bbc.co.uk
Provides a free catalogue for learning programmes including languages.

The Open University
0870 3330087
www.open.ac.uk
Offers chances to study for a degree by distance learning.

U3A (University of The Third Age)
020 7837 8838
www.u3a.org.uk
Your local branch will be in the telephone directory.
Offers a wide variety of study courses.

National Extension College
01223 450200
www.nec.ac.uk

Open College for the Arts
01226 730495
www.oca-uk.com
For studies in the creative arts.

Websites
For information on foster-grandparenting:
www.urbanext.uiuc.edu
www.metfamily.org

For online tutorials:
www.idf50.co.uk/internettutorials.htm
www.itsonline.com
www.cires.colorado.edu

For information on Lifelong Learning:
www.con-ed.cam.ac.uk

Brain power

Recommended reading
Dr Dharma Singh Khalsa, *The Mind Miracle* (Arrow, 1997)
For an inspiring read on brain health
Tony Buzan and Raymond Keene, *The Age Heresy* (Ebury, 1996)
Susan Greenfield, *The Human Brain* (Weidenfeld and Nicolson 1997)

Contacts
Lamberts mail order
01892 554312
Supply gingko and gingseng and many other supplements.

Websites
To do a personality test:
www.kiersey.com
www.geocities.com

Love is all there is

Recommended reading
Dorothy Rowe, *The Successful Self* (Collins, 1988)
Sheila Kitzinger, *Woman's Experience of Sex* (Dorling Kindersley, 1993)
Jean Shapiro, *Get the Best out of the Rest of your Life* (Thorsons, 1990)

Websites
Websites for carers:
www.helptheaged.org.uk
www.ageconcern.org.uk
www.50plus.org

Skilful beauty care

Recommended reading
Deborah Hutton, *Vogue Futures* (Condé Nast, 1994)
Jo Fairley and Sarah Stacey, *Feel Fabulous Forever* (Kyle Cathie, 1999)

Contact
Fragrant Earth
01458 831216
www.fragrant-earth.com
For base oils, creams, lanolin, beeswax and essential oils.

Vital health

Recommended reading

Lynne Robinson and Gordon Thomson, *Body Control the Pilates Way* (Pan, 1998)
Peter West, *Biorhythms* (Element, 1999)

Contacts

Iyengar Yoga Centre London
020 7624 3080
www.iyi.org.uk

British Wheel of Yoga
01529 306851
www.bwy.org.uk

Sivananda Centre London
020 8780 0160
www.sivananada.org

Pilates Studio, London
020 7584 4898
www.pilates-studio.com

Menopause

Recommended reading

Germaine Greer, *The Change* (Hamish Hamilton, 1991)
Marilyn Glenville, *Natural Alternatives to HRT* (Kyle Cathie, 1999)

NHS handouts in bone-density clinics give excellent advice on menopause.

Money matters

Recommended reading

Choose from a number of financial magazines on the shelf (*The Economist, Investor*) and read the *Financial Times* as well as financial pages of the broadsheets.

Websites

www.arp.org
www.moneyextra.com
www.saga.co.uk
www.ageconcern.org.uk
www.willswizard.com

Play it safe

Recommended reading

Your Practical Guide to Crime Prevention published by the Home Office is available from your local police station.

Contact

Victim Support
01223 329000 (for central address and website)

Enjoy yourself

Recommended reading

Julia Cameron, *The Artist's Way* (Pan, 1994)
Stafford Whiteaker, *The Good Retreat Guide* (Rider, 1998)

Contacts

Saga Holidays
0800 300456
www.saga.co.uk
www.ageconcern.org.uk

ACE (Association for Cultural Exchange)
01223 835055
www.study-tours.org

Websites

www.vavo.com
www.idf50.co.uk (I Don't Feel Fifty!)
www.livingto100.com
www.theoldie.co.uk
www.thirdage.com
www.arp.org.uk

Further reading

Rosamond Richardson, *Natural Superwoman* (Kyle Cathie 1999)
Naomi Wolf, *The Beauty Myth* (Vintage 1991)
John Berger, *Ways of Seeing* (Penguin 1972)
Lynne Segal, *Is the Future Female?* (Vintage 1988)
Mae West, *Goodness has nothing to do with it* (Vintage 1996)

index